A HISTORY OF
WOMEN'S CONTRIBUTION
TO WORLD HEALTH

Theodora P. Dakin

Studies in Health and Human Services
Volume 21

The Edwin Mellen Press
Lewiston/Queenston/Lampeter

R.
692
D34
1992

Library of Congress Cataloging-in-Publication Data

Dakin, Theodora P.
    A history of women's contribution to world health / Theodora P.
Dakin.
        p.   cm. -- (Studies in health and human services ; v. 21)
    Includes bibliographical references and index.
    ISBN 0-7734-9624-6
    1. Women in medicine--History. I. Title. II. Series.
    [DNLM: 1. History of Medicine. 2. Women history. 3. World
Health. W1 ST92D v. 21 / WZ80.5.W5 D135h]
    R692.D34   1992
    610'.82--dc20
    DNLM/DLC
    for Library of Congress   91-46383
                                                      CIP

This is volume 21 in the continuing series
Studies in Health and Human Services
Volume 21 ISBN 0-7734-9624-6
SHHS Series ISBN 0-88946-126-0

The Edwin Mellen Press   The Edwin Mellen Press
Box 450   Box 67
Lewiston, NY 14092   Queenston, Ontario
USA   CANADA, L0S 1L0

The Edwin Mellen Press, Ltd.
Lampeter, Dyfed, Wales
UNITED KINGDOM SA48 7DY

Printed in the United States of America

To Emily Dakin, my granddaughter

Contents

	page
Foreword	i
Introduction	iii
1. Dawn of Civilization through Classical Greece Pre-146 BC	1
2. The Roman Era 146 BC-AD 499	7
3. The Middle Ages 500-1399	11
4. The Renaissance 1400-1699	19
5. The Age of Enlightenment 1700-1799	27
6. Industrial, Social, and Scientific Revolutions 1800-1849	35
7. War and Social Conscience 1850-1874	43
8. Growth and Expansion 1875-1899	53
9. The Twentieth Century Begins 1900-1924	63
10. Economic Depression through the Atomic Age 1925-1949	77
11. Feminism Comes of Age 1950-1975	87
Bibliography	97
Biographical Index	105
Index	109

Foreword

I want to express my gratitude to the many people who have encouraged me as I worked on this project, prodded me when I wanted to give it up, and nudged me to bring it to completion. To mention a few: my husband Tom who encouraged me to become involved with the computer, without which I never would have persevered; my children Priscilla and Jim who urged me to complete it; Gladys Vandenbelt, who suggested the appropriate women to include; Debbie Farkas, who suggested the source material; Marion Loveday, who suggested an appropriate publisher; Ann Wagstaff, Lois Arntzen and my many Murrysville friends who continually asked me when the book would be completed. I am especially grateful to Cindy Walker, who created order out of chaos.

Introduction

Throughout history women have played a pivotal role in the general health care of their society. Often these women have overcome tremendous hardships to achieve their goals and many times were forced to challenge a culture or government that had placed on them unreasonable restraints. Typically women have been held to a higher standard than men and usually did so for little or no pay–certainly always at a lower salary than their male counterparts. Through sheer determination though, they all surpassed the obstacles placed before them, and most were able to achieve their goals.

This book is not intended to be an examination of world history or an exploration of medical achievements. Rather, it is meant to illustrate the contributions women have made to the development of world health. And there have been many. Rarely are women's accomplishments included in the history of a society or culture. In most instances, women have assumed the caretaker role–tending to the home and family and rarely venturing into the world of science. When the needs of women, children, the poor, and the handicapped were not adequately met, however, it was the women who stepped in and used their own unique abilities to affect change. They often faced social and professional ostracism but proved that they could perform successfully–often with a family to care for as well.

Events in history have also profoundly influenced medicine and health care. Many great scientific discoveries have been made under the duress of war or epidemic. But even in times of war, women did not shirk their responsibility to help the less fortunate. They bravely faced the challenges of the battlefield and provided needed care for wounded soldiers. Few, however, have been recognized for their efforts.

The women included in this compendium come from different social and educational backgrounds, but it is interesting to note that many had a father, brother, husband, or other male influence who encouraged their pursuits. All of the women here have impacted the field of health care in some way, and many were not physicians. Until recently, women have usually been barred from obtaining a medical degree, so many had to find other ways in which to serve and some opened up new areas of health care altogether. They all publicized their efforts and little by little they began to open up the world of medicine and science to future generations of women.

This book ends in the year 1975. By that time it was clear that as women were allowed to participate in the health field, they would make important contributions. Because of the efforts of the women presented here, today's women are actively participating in the general scientific and medical fields.

TPD

Chapter 1

Dawn of Civilization through Classical Greece
Pre-146 BC

The idea of treating and caring for the sick didn't come about at any one particular time in history. Instead, health care evolved at varying rates over many centuries. While little is known of the medical approaches used by primitive man, there is some evidence to suggest that simple wounds were treated either by sewing them closed or by applying various concoctions to the afflicted area.[1] Whether women were involved in medical treatment is unknown, but throughout history women have usually assumed the nurturing duties, so they may have been important health care providers.

It wasn't until the early Egyptians began documenting their activities that a clear picture of ancient health care practices became available. In Egypt's Valley of Tombs of the Kings intricate pictographic portrayals of Egyptian life are found on the walls inside the great pyramids. Within one of the pyramids is a depiction of Merit Ptah (ca. 2500 BC), who is the first female physician of record.[2]

But Merit Ptah wasn't the only woman to attend the early medical schools. Egyptian women shared equal status with men and were trained as physicians and surgeons. Women interested in obstetrics and gynecology could attend the women's medical school at the Temple of Sais, on the Rosetta Mouth of the Nile.[3]

Egyptian culture by 2500 BC was well structured and most citizens were well educated. Boys and girls attended school and were given a solid grounding in government and the sciences. Meanwhile, philosophers, teachers, and scribes pondered the relationship of man and his universe as the fields of science and mathematics flourished. Principals of irrigation and engineering were developed to enrich the soil beyond the Nile River Valley and helped provide farmers with abundant crops. In the cities, merchants and craftsmen thrived, while artisans and architects created great buildings and monuments.[4]

Health care in Egypt was a complex mix of religion and sorcery combined with primitive remedies and techniques. Egyptian physicians probably relied on one medical text, the *Ebers Papyrus*, which dates back to 1500 BC. Spells and incantations were performed to cure patients' ills. Remedies for fevers, infections, eye diseases, and crocodile bites are chronicled in the text, but little information was provided about the specific needs of women.[5] The Egyptians were known for their knowledge of diagnosis and treatment of some diseases. Simple fractures were treated, and primitive surgical techniques were often successful. While medicine often relied on superstition and the occult to promote healing, some physicians had an impressive understanding of anatomy and pathology. "Unlike some peoples of a later date they ascribed disease to natural causes. They discovered the value of cathartics, noted the curative properties of numerous drugs, and compiled the first *materia medica*, or catalogue of medicines."[6]

Still, life expectancy for the average Egyptian was not long and most expected to be rewarded with a glorious life after death. They concentrated their efforts on making the journey into the hereafter pleasant by developing intricate embalming methods and building elaborate tombs to prepare the deceased for the afterlife.[7]

Religion in early Egypt centered around Re, the sun god of righteousness, justice, truth, and the moral order of the universe. Later, Amen became chief god under Re and continuously vied for supremacy over Orisis, who eventually symbolized immortality. Other subordinate deities were also worshipped and consulted for divine intervention.[8] Matters of fertility and motherhood, however, were relegated to the goddess Isis.[9]

Generally, issues involving fertility and maternity were brought to the attention of the goddesses, while more serious health matters were left to the masculine deities. Unlike the divine gods and goddesses of Egypt, the early

Greeks consulted various supernatural gods and goddesses to remedy ailments and cure diseases. Diana, for example, was thought to be capable of treating all diseases of women; Eileithyia was the great goddess of childbirth; and Persephone was responsible for relieving pain. But, it was the daughters of Aesculapius, Hygieia and Panaceia, who were associated with healing. Whether she was truly a goddess, or merely a talented mortal, Hygieia is known to have been a practicing physician. Little is known about her sister, Panaceia, but her name continues to be associated with curing all ills and difficulties.[10]

As Greek culture evolved and small village communities grew into large city-states, the development of a great society was taking shape. Women played a significant role in health care and, as in Egypt, were accepted as physicians and healers. Women were known to hold positions as professors of medicine and to have written medical texts.[11]

But, perhaps, the greatest contributions of classical Greece were those of the great philosophers. "The major Greek philosophers raised all the great issues of life, living and death, most of which remain unanswered." Socrates, Plato, and Hippocrates all advanced ideas about the universe, man, and nature. Through the work of Hippocrates of Cos (ca. 1500 BC), medicine advanced at a remarkable pace. Considered the father of medicine, he was responsible for the idea that all disease is as a result of a natural cause. The Hippocratic oath established a code of ethics that is still part of the basic philosophy of Western physicians, and his careful clinical records reveal a common-sense, natural approach to health, which stressed a balanced diet and rest, combined with an understanding of personal hygiene.[12]

As Greek civilization developed, the political and social roles of women were denigrated, and by the sixth century BC, most women were relegated to a subservient status. Women with personal medical problems did not consult physicians, and they were strictly forbidden to practice medicine. Perhaps it was seeing many women die needlessly in childbirth that prompted Agnodice (fl. 506 BC) to disguise herself as a man in order to learn and then to specialize in obstetrics and gynecology. Female patients, knowing her true identity, preferred her care to that of her male counterparts and supported her efforts. Her ability to attract female patients aroused the suspicions of some of her colleagues, and eventually she was arrested for malpractice. At her trial she shocked the court by revealing her true identity. Throngs of women rallied to her side and created such a protest that the law banning women practitioners was abolished.[13,14,15]

Later, Aristotle (384-322 BC), a physician and philosopher, confused science by expounding a philosophic approach to health and medical problems. There is evidence, however, that cases of trauma, especially fractures, were dealt with logically and sometimes successfully. Patients who suffered soft-tissue wounds, however, had a high fatality rate of 70% or more, because of the potential for infection and hemorrhage. Aristotle's philosophic approach to general medical care and the unsuccessful treatment of wounds continued until the second century BC.[16]

As Greek culture was reaching maturity, political leaders were becoming nervous: Rome, a distant, but aggressive civilization, was advancing throughout the western world conquering most of Europe, Egypt, and parts of Asia. The Achaean League of Greek States was formed to fend off the hostile invaders. The coalition put up a brave defense, but was badly defeated in 146 BC.[17]

As the Roman Empire grew and the glory of countries, such as Egypt and Greece, faded, the world's social and political center shifted to Rome. Physicians were brought from Greece to the capital city and brought new medical ideas with them. The Romans, however, had not experienced healing by physicians before and some were skeptical. "The doctors received a mixed welcome, being approved by some and abhorred by others. In general, however, their status slowly improved."[18]

Endnotes Chapter 1

1. Philip Rhodes, *An Outline History of Medicine*, p. 6.

2. Marjorie P. K. Weiser and Jean S. Arbeiter, *Womanlist*, p. 137.

3. Geoffrey Marks and William K. Beatty, *Women in White*, pp. 41-42.

4. Walther Kirchner, *Western Civilization to 1500*, pp. 6-9.

5. Rhodes, *An Outline History of Medicine*, p. 8.

6. Edward McNall Burns and Philip Lee Ralph, *et al.*, *World Civilizations*, 6th ed., p. 35.

7. Rhodes, *An Outline History of Medicine*, p. 9.

8. Burns and Ralph, *et al.*, *World Civilizations*, 6th ed., pp. 30-31.

9. Kirchner, *Western Civilization to 1500*, p. 10.

10. Marks and Beatty, *Women in White*, pp. 38-39.

11. Robert Flaceliere, *Daily Life in Greece at the time of Pericles*, trans. Peter Green, p. 144

12. Rhodes, *An Outline History of Medicine*, p. 11.

13. Marks and Beatty, Women in White, p. 42.

14. Jennifer S. Uglow, ed., *The International Dictionary of Women's Biography*, p. 7.

15. Judy Chicago, *The Dinner Party*, p. 123.

16. Burns and Ralph, *et al.*, *World Civilizations*, 6th ed., p. 193.

17. Kirchner, *Western Civilization to 1500*, p. 95.

18. Rhodes, *An Outline History of Medicine*, p. 19.

Chapter 2

The Roman Era
146 BC-AD 499

The Romans had conquered much of the regions to their east, west, and north by the time they finally defeated the Achaean League in the middle of the second century BC. It was the Greeks, however, who shared many aspects of their culture and scientific knowledge with their captors. But the Romans were more interested in military science than medical science and the latter suffered during this period. Medical treatment included appealing to the appropriate goddess for aid, with many donations of seemingly appropriate gifts. Minerva, for example, was known as the great healer and was responsible for all intellectual and academic activity. The goddess Diana was thought to be capable of treating diseases in women. Those who wanted children consulted the "good goddess," Bona Dea, or the goddess of good fortune, Fortuna.

One physician who moved to Rome from Pergamum Greece, however, had a profound effect on the future of medicine. Galen (AD 120-201), a physician and medical writer, wrote prolifically, but his authoritarian and autocratic beliefs lacked a sound scientific basis. He believed the human body was an instrument for the souls–a philosophy that suited the Christian, Hebrew, and Arabic religions. While his physiologic expositions were based on Aristotle's philosophy, his knowledge of the anatomy was far superior to any previous physician. While his treatment of disease was limited to diet, a few drugs chosen empirically, and bathing, his teachings persisted unchallenged until the early Renaissance period.[1]

Innovations in public hygiene improved general health care, although done without intention. The idea of sanitary engineering was developed as swamps were drained, water supply facilities erected, public baths built, and sewer systems installed.

As the society became more sophisticated and the Greek influence more prominent, the role of women also changed to include a voice in government and also the ability to serve as physicians and teachers. Cleopatra (ca. AD 100) was an obstetrician and gynecologist. Her vast knowledge led her to write extensively about women's health matters, and some evidence suggests that her work may have been used for centuries by men who refused to give her credit for her work.[2]

Women made important contributions by teaching in ancient Rome. Metrodora (fl. 2nd c.) was a physician concerned with women's issues and wrote what has become the oldest medical manual written by a woman that is still in existence. Her concern with diseases of the uterus is evident throughout the 263-page manual, which also contained prescriptions for treating diseases of the stomach, uterus, and kidneys.[3,4]

Surgeons, however, did not share the same status as physicians and teachers. Aspasia (ca. 2nd c.) specialized in the surgical treatment of obstetric and gynecologic problems. She was skilled in podalic version, a method of repositioning the fetus within the womb, diagnosis of fetal positions, and the treatment of painful menstruation. Women who sought her advice were subjected to admonitions for preventing abortion, but also were given suggestions on inducing abortions when necessary. She advised on potential dangers to the mother and subsequent care of aborted fetuses.[5]

It was around this time that Rome began a slow decline as a new and powerful movement, called Christianity, began to sweep the society. Fabiola (d. 399) was one of the first members of the noble classes to accept the teachings of the Christian church. Although she had defied convention when, at age 20 she divorced her first husband, it still must have been a shock to find a once noble woman giving up everything to minister to the sick and dying. She was one of 15 women who followed the direction of St. Jerome by offering her services free to the indigent. After the death of her second husband, she struggled, along with others, to form a distinctly female order of Christian ministry. In 370, Fabiola opened Rome's first public hospital, called Nosocomium, to care for the sick and indigent. The patients who sought care at the hospital were often surprised to see Fabiola acting as physician and nurse, as well as teaching Christian doctrine. Her charitable contributions were also widely known. Her reputation was so widespread that upon her death, thousands of mourners converged on the capital city to pay their respects.[6,7]

Christianity spread widely throughout the Roman Empire and eventually became the state religion under the reigns of Constantine and Theodosius (ca. 312). Clearly, attitudes were changing in the Roman culture, particularly those dealing with women and marriage. Women, who had been treated as second-class citizens, were now "regarded as being equal to male[s] in the eyes of God." However, marriage was seen only as a vehicle for procreation and women were expected to be subservient to their husbands. "Even though they had full hopes for salvation, they were treated as inferiors in the everyday affairs of the world."[8]

And worldly affairs must have weighed heavily on the minds of Christian men of the Roman Empire. To the North, Germany was making hostile moves against the Empire. Finally, one aggressive tribe, the Visigoths, sacked the Roman Empire between 410-455, and the torch of civilization was passed to the Eastern Empires, Byzantium and the Arabs.

Endnotes Chapter 2

1. Rhodes, *An Outline History of Medicine,* p. 21.

2. Joan Macksey and Kenneth Macksey, *The Book of Women's Achievements*, p. 140.

3. Marilyn Bailey Ogilvie, *Women in Science*, p. 132.

4. Chicago, *The Dinner Party*, p. 127.

5. Ogilvie, *Women in Science,* p. 32.

6. *Ibid.*, p. 83.

7. Chicago, *The Dinner Party*, p. 130.

8. Burns and Ralph, *et al., World Civilizations*, 6th ed., pp. 287-288.

Chapter 3

The Middle Ages
500-1399

The years 500 to 1399 represent a long period of confusion in the Western world–political power shifted, cultural centers changed, there were many devastating wars, and pestilence raged uncontrolled.

With the fall of the Roman Empire to the Visigoths, Europe plunged into the Middle Ages. The cultural and commercial centers shifted to the Byzantine Empire in Constantinople (Istanbul), and the Islamic territory of Persia (Iran).

Constantinople bustled with activity in the sixth century and great advances, including the codification of Roman law, were made under the leadership of Justinian (527-563) and his wife, Theodora (508-548). She was unlike her predecessors and was known for her astute character and determination.[1] She was also known for presumptuous behavior. "No princess of the royal blood ever wore her crown more arrogantly than [Theodora]."[2] However, Theodora also was diligent in her beliefs and was responsible for enacting laws to advance the interests of women.[3]

Religion dominated Byzantine society, and although they practiced Christianity, the citizens also preserved many of the Greek traditions. The status of women had improved, and wealthy families encouraged education for both boys and girls. Girls, however, were kept at home and were taught by private tutors, but they were allowed to earn medical educations and practice medicine.[4]

All the medical education available at the time, however, couldn't have prepared anyone for the devastation that occurred after the start of the world-wide plague in 542. Beginning in Lower Egypt, the disease, thought to be Bubonic Plague, spread quickly through Alexandria and Palestine. Initially, the mortality rate from the disease was low in Constantinople, but soon the death rate rose until 10,000 people died each day from the disease. "So many were the deaths that graves could not be dug sufficiently quickly. Roofs were taken off the towers of forts, the towers filled with corpses and the roofs replaced. Ships were loaded with the dead, rowed out to sea and abandoned."[5]

As the world struggled with this destructive disease, the Arabs were having the greatest effect on science and medicine, with the new scientific center now in Baghdad. A new religious movement was gaining momentum so that by the seventh century, Islam had begun to have a profound effect on world history as it spread through the Middle East, Egypt, and Spain. Founded by the prophet Mohammed (570-632), this new religion was based on the belief that one should completely submit to God's will. "[Mohammed] had come to profess one God and, as his prophet, to preach a life of righteousness on earth and to promise an eternal bliss for the pure after death."[6]

Muslim rule spread throughout parts of Europe and the Middle East. As they conquered new territories, they discovered new methods of healing. They were devoted to learning and initiated a new era which vigorously pursued scientific knowledge. They were responsible for translating many texts in Arabic and, from there, went on to advance their own new theories on health care.

The Arabs continued to dominate the scientific scene throughout the eighth and ninth centuries. One physician, Rhazes of Basra (860-932), was the first to recognize smallpox, plague, consumption, and rabies, as infectious diseases. In addition, Islamic scientists discovered the value of cauterization, were able to identify poisons and prescribe antidotes, and made major advances in treating diseases of the eye.

The Muslims excelled all other medieval peoples in the organization of hospitals and in the control of medical practice. Each had wards for particular cases, a dispensary, and a library. The chief physicians and surgeons lectured to the students and graduates, examined them, and issued licenses to practice. Even the owners of leeches, who in most cases were also barbers, had to submit them for inspection at regular intervals.[7]

While the Arabs were investing their energies in scientific endeavors, the Western Christian civilization was lagging far behind. "Material conditions throughout this period were so primitive that we can almost speak of five centuries of camping-out."[8] Changes began to take place around 800–the most significant being the coronation of Charlemagne (768-814) as the first Holy Roman Emperor. Charlemagne conquered most of western Europe and sparked a new "renaissance" in the region. "In monasteries and palace schools, classical texts were once more studied, theological problems pondered, books collected, and manuscripts copied." Scholarly pursuits were encouraged, and the arts were revitalized.[9] But Charlemagne's goal of uniting Europe was short-lived. After his death, the empire was divided among his grandsons. It wasn't until the tenth century that Otto the Great was able to rebuild the empire in the tradition of Charlemagne.

By that time, the center of great medical knowledge and achievements had shifted from the Middle East to Italy. At the beginning of the tenth century, a great independent medical school was founded at Salerno, Italy. This marked the first time an organized system of medical study was developed. The practice of medicine was taken out of the hands of the church and put back into the hands of the laity. Teaching was still based on the tenets of Hippocrates, Galen, and Aristotle, but was enriched by a blending of Greek, Roman, and Hebrew knowledge. Students were required to be at least age 21 at the time of entrance and had to pass certain examinations to be admitted to the five-year course of study.[10]

Students of the coeducational Salerno Medical School most likely studied obstetrics and gynecology under Trotula Platerius (1050-1097). She was a professor who wrote the first book by a Christian author on obstetrics and women's health, *On Diseases of Women*. Problems of menstruation, sterility, and pediatrics were dealt with in a practical manner. Chapters offered advice on signs of pregnancy, difficult parturition, infant feedings, choice of nurse, and care of the newborn. Treatments were suggested for cough, dysentery, stone, ulcer, pediculi, swollen glands, fistulae, cancer, uterine polyps, epilepsy, and diseases of the teeth and gums. Trotula also stressed the importance of hygiene, cleanliness, and exercise.[11]

As students undertook the study of medicine in Salerno, much of the Western world was becoming completely absorbed in the Crusades (1096-1303). A new religious fervor had developed as thousands of men, women, and children set off from Europe to wrest Jerusalem from the infidels. Inadequately prepared for the ordeal, however, large numbers of people died by drowning, and from battle wounds and disease. Those who survived returned to Europe only to spread leprosy, plague, tuberculosis, tetanus, and dysentery. Medical ignorance, inadequate health facilities, deplorable health and hygiene habits, as well as poor living conditions merely compounded the problem.

Hospitals, many directed and staffed by Byzantine women, began to emerge to care for the sick and wounded Crusaders. Anna Comnena (1083-1148), daughter of King Alexis I, was one of the outstanding physicians of her time who contributed her services to those who had been wounded in battle. After studying all that was known of medicine at that time, she wrote a treatise on gout which was a common disorder at the time. She practiced in all of the hospitals and orphan asylums in Constantinople, including the 10,000-bed hospital her father had constructed. As she visited the sick and dying, she kept a diary of the appearance and daily actions of the hordes of pilgrims who arrived in Constantinople's hospitals. At the time of her father's death, her husband, Nicephorus Byennius, tried unsuccessfully to have Anna assume the throne, rather than her brother John. After her husband's death, Anna entered a monastery and devoted her life to writing *Alexiad*, a 15-volume epic poem on the history of her father's reign, providing a valuable source of information about the time.[12]

By now, medical knowledge had reached a standstill in Europe, with treatments consisting of empiric spells. Charms, herbs, diet, and inappropriate medications, such as pulverized pearls and opiates, prevailed. Surgery was attempted, but often impeded by inaccurate knowledge of anatomy and ignorance of hygiene. Frantic, ignorant fear led to ineffective solutions to medical problems. Folklore, religious fervor, psychic disturbances, and dependence on fetishes developed as the sick or injured tried to cope with their disorders. Living conditions were deplorable for everyone and many took refuge in the convents and monasteries, which served as the reservoirs of culture. Hospitals were built under the auspices of the church and were often administered and staffed by women.

In one small nunnery attached to the cloister of Disbodenberg in Germany, an 8-year-old girl, who was later to have a profound influence on health care, entered the convent. Hildegard of Bingen (1099-1179), considered to be the first medical writer in Germany, was age 37 when she became abbess of the cloister she had joined at such a young age. Ten years later, she founded her own convent in Rupertsburg, which became the spiritual center to which popes, kings, and ecclesiastical and secular dignitaries turned for advice.[13]

She wrote 14 books, in all, some of them in several volumes. *Physica* discussed plants, trees, animals, stones, metals, and elements which held medicinal value for humans. Her source for information was folk medicine and popular tradition, but she also had practical knowledge of over 485 plants and drugs. *Liber Compositae Medicinae* concerned the nature, form, and cause of disease. Her studies covered the entire life spectrum from embryology to decay. She discussed headaches, vertigo, brain fever, heart pain due to gas in the stomach, coughs, gout, jaundice, dysentery, diseases of the kidney and bladder and their diagnosis by the appearance of urine. She had passages on hygiene during pregnancy and rules for suppressing sexual desires. *Liber Divinorum Oiperum* contained 187 chapters and discussed anatomy, physiology, and the atmospheric conditions that caused disease. Large amounts of milk or water, sleep, exercise, and the avoidance of beer and wine were all recommended. Although her theories were a mix of religion, Aristotelian philosophy, astrology, alchemy, and folklore, her advice was influenced by her spiritual visions resulting in the inseparability of the physical and spiritual. "Hildegard foreshadowed such later discoveries as the circulation of the blood, the causes of contagion and of autointoxication, nerve action originating in the brain, and the chemistry of the blood.[14]

New ideas were developing in the Western world, however, and medical knowledge was increasing. Oxford University was founded in

England in 1167, and Paris University gradually evolved after 1231. Marco Polo had introduced new ideas about life inside China when he wrote *Travels with Marco Polo* in 1295. And, Chaucer was presenting his views in his books in the late fourteenth century.

But new ideas about medicine still couldn't stop the ravages of disease. In 1347, bubonic plague, better known as "The Black Death," spread throughout Europe leaving 60,000,000 people dead. Other scourges included St. Vitus' Dance, leprosy, tuberculosis, tetanus, dysentery, gangrene, influenza, and scurvy.[15]

In 1352, women were granted the right to practice medicine when King John of France prohibited medical practice by anyone other than a specially trained physician. Only those students who had received diplomas from universities were allowed to practice. Since Italian universities were the only ones to admit women at the time, few women qualified for the honor. The Catholic church later remanded this law and specifically prohibited the practice of medicine by women.[16]

Endnotes Chapter 3

1. Burns and Ralph, *et al., World Civilizations*, 6th ed., p. 298.

2. Henry Thomas and Dana Lee Thomas, *Living Biographies of Famous Women*, p. 24.

3. *Ibid.*, p. 27.

4. Burns and Ralph, *et al., World Civilizations*, 6th ed., p. 365.

5. Frederick F. Cartwright, *Disease and History*, p. 17.

6. Kirchner, *Western Civilization to 1500,* p. 152.

7. Burns and Ralph, *et al., World Civilizations*, 6th ed., p. 381.

8. *Ibid.*, p. 386.

9. Kirchner, *Western Civilization to 1500*, p. 161.

10. Kenneth Walker, *The Story of Medicine*, p. 75.

11. Macksey and Macksey, *The Book of Women's Achievements*, p. 141.

12. Uglow, ed., *The International Dictionary of Women's Biography*, p. 120.

13. Marks and Beatty, *Women in White*, p. 48.

14. *Ibid.*, p. 49.

15. Brian Inglis, *A History of Medicine*, p. 64.

16. Marks and Beatty, *Women in White*, p. 55.

Chapter 4

The Renaissance
1400-1699

The fifteenth century marked the beginning of an exciting era of innovation and advancement known as the Renaissance. Science–particularly astronomy and physics–challenged conventional Church doctrine, and new ideas of nature and the universe were espoused. The church, however, was unprepared for the turmoil created by this new way of thinking.

> Whereas the clergy had, almost by default, arrogated to themselves exclusive rights to all knowledge, they were now being shown that there were certain spheres in which their total remit did not run. As a result there could be thought, observation, and later experiment, unconstrained by dogmatic theology.[1]

The fact that the views of the Church were being questioned did not mean that people were turning away from their religious beliefs. Rather, splinter religious groups were being established to pursue their own interpretations of religion.

This new era, which encouraged exploration of traditional thinking, was the dawn of the modern age. Education flourished and a proliferation of independent colleges began to spring up throughout Europe. Leipzig University in Germany was founded in 1409, while Eton and King's College, in Cambridge, England, were both founded in 1441. New techniques in tool-making led to new inventions. Artists and craftsmen found innovative ways to express themselves.

But as all these extraordinary changes took place, fundamentally little changed for women. In 1421, the Church issued an edict forbidding women to practice medicine or perform surgery. Italian universities, however, had always been more receptive to women students, and despite the Church's orders, Lauria Constantia Calenda (fl. 15th c.) was one of the few women physicians to graduate from Salerno (Italy) University, and she made a great reputation for herself.[2]

One woman to champion the cause of freedom and independence for women was Christine de Pizan (1363-1431). Considered to be the first professional writer, she wrote books and articles advocating equality for women and stressing the need for their education in law, medicine, and finance. A recurring theme in many of her works is the inaccessibility of education to most women. Her father, an Italian physician who was appointed to the position of court astrologer to Charles V of France, encouraged Christine's education. Her father's position in the court enabled her to receive a good education a unique opportunity for a woman of her generation. She married at age 15, but her husband died when she was 25, leaving her with three small children to support, so Christine used her education and talents to become an accomplished writer and lyric poet. In 1405 she published her best-known work *Le livre de la cité des dames (The Book of the City of Ladies)*, which describes a mythological city consisting of the greatest women of all eras and social classes. She was the official biographer of Charles V, and, in 1429, she wrote *Le Dirie sur Jehanne d'Arc*, the only work to honor Joan of Arc. In all, she produced over 20 works on subjects as diverse as poetry, politics, and an instruction manual for knights. "Between 1390 and 1429 she produced a vast corpus of works in verse and prose, whose range shows a technical mastery of the various well-established literary genres of her day and demonstrates an astonishing poetic versatility."[3]

Perhaps the most important development during the Renaissance was the introduction of movable type in the mid-1400's by Johann Gutenberg. Not only did this new process allow the Bible to be mass produced, it also encouraged the spread of ideas through books, pamphlets, and newspapers.

Expression of new ideas was discouraged by the Church. To counter the advances that were being made and the changes that were occurring in the Church, Spain's King Ferdinand and Queen Isabella initiated the Inquisition of 1480, which resulted in the deaths of 2,000 people who had been found guilty of heresy against the Church.

During this period, an increasing knowledge of the world beyond Europe was sparking a new age of discovery. Christopher Columbus sailed to the New World in 1492; Vasco da Gama rounded the Cape of Good Hope in 1497, and in 1519, Ferdinand Magellan's ship circumnavigated the world.

Medicine also progressed at a rapid pace. Galen's teachings, Aristotle's philosophy, and church domination were all being contested. In 1530, Paracelsus (1493-1541) wrote the first manual of surgery, *Die gross Wundartzney, (Great Surgery Book)* and introduced the use of chemicals into medical practice. He was also the first to describe manifestations of syphilis and to use mercury as a treatment for the disease. Matters of health were becoming so significant that by 1538, Henry VIII ordered that records be kept of christenings, marriages, and deaths. In 1540, Miguel Servetus described the pulmonary circulation of blood. In 1543, Andreas Vesalius published a landmark book, *De Fabrica Corporis,* which was the first book of human anatomy and was based on his observations of numerous dissections. The book, which refuted many of Galen's teachings and put anatomy on a firm, realistic basis, was produced on a printing press and, therefore, available to all. The fear of infections and disease were constant during the Renaissance period. In 1546, Hieronymus Fracastorius suggested that infectious disease might be caused by living organisms that were transmitted from person to person.[4,5]

Others in the field of medicine and health care were also making advances. Ambroise Pare (1510-1590) wrote a treatise on the treatment of gunshot wounds, which advocated the ligature of blood vessels, closure of wounds, and a protective covering, rather than the more common treatment of hot oil and cautery. He suggested less destructive surgery than was commonly practiced and reintroduced a version of extraction as a life-saving measure in difficult deliveries[6]

Interest in the universe continued to capture the attention of scientists and philosophers. By now Copernicus had introduced the radical notion that the earth and other planets rotated around the sun, rather than the Church's claim that the sun circled the planets. Galileo (1564-1610), using a telescope, corroborated this theory and was deemed a heretic by the Church. He also pioneered theories of gravitation and motion, which lay the groundwork for Isaac Newton's theories of physical law.

Culture and the arts blossomed during the sixteenth century. In 1559, Elizabeth I was crowned and a brilliant cultural period developed in England. In Italy, the arts thrived under the sponsorship of the Medicis. Leonardo da Vinci and Michelangelo produced their great works during this era and were influential throughout the world with their ideas and realistic portrayals of the human body.

Despite these new ideas and spectacular developments, serious problems persisted. Overwhelming health problems continued to plague Europe during the Renaissance. In the sixteenth century, the average duration of life was 18 years. Half of the inhabitants of Europe died before their 12th year, and 60% of these died before their fifth birthday. Plague epidemics frequently spread through Europe. Influenza epidemics and a virulent syphilis epidemic also spread throughout Europe and were especially devastating in the sixteenth and seventeenth centuries. Other serious diseases persisted and claimed thousands of lives; measles, scarlet fever, plague, tuberculosis, pneumonia, scabies, scurvy, tetanus, dysentery, child-bed fever, and smallpox were commonplace. And all were aggravated by lack of knowledge of proper hygiene, irrational and often harmful therapy, abysmally inadequate housing, crowded living conditions and improper diet.[7]

Obstetrics suffered greatly during this period, since the teachings of Trotula and previous midwives were forgotten. The delivery of infants was relegated to ignorant and untrained midwives and was basically a matter of watchful waiting in squalid locations.

Louise Bourgeois (1553-1636), however, combined her training, skill, and determination to improve the state of women's health. After completing her training under Pare she became midwife to Queen Marie D'Medici of France. Widely known for her caution and skill, she became an authority on podalic version and was the first to force premature labor in cases of severe hemorrhaging. In 1609, she published *Observations*, which discussed sterility, fertility, childbirth, diseases of women, care of the newborn, and resuscitation of a seemingly lifeless infant. The book also provided detailed information about the female anatomy, stages of pregnancy, and treatment for abnormalities of labor. So knowledgeable and well respected was she that in 1635 the midwives of Paris requested that she present a public course in obstetrics. Much to their dismay, however, the Paris Faculty of Medicine refused to grant their permission for such a gathering.[8,9]

Prevention of maternal and infant mortality was one concern of Queen Sophia (fl. 16th c.) of Scandinavia. She was instrumental in instituting health care reforms in Denmark and Norway following the death of her husband. To reduce the high death rate from childbirth, she advocated birth control measures and less frequent pregnancies. She established strict rules to be followed at the birth of a baby: only a specially trained midwife, the nurse, and the husband could be present at the delivery. Sanitation rules were established and included frequent bathing, isolation of sick patients, fumigation of head lice, disposal of bodies which died of plague, and open windows at night.[10]

In most cases, care of the indigent or handicapped was left to sisters of the Church. Humanitarian efforts, however, were gaining momentum in the early seventeenth century. In 1629, Louise de Marillac (1591-1661) assisted Vincent de Paul in organizing the Daughters of Charity–the first organization of women nurses to officially work with doctors in the care of the sick. Founded by a group of religious women, the organization was dedicated to serving institutions for the poor and handicapped, caring for foundlings and orphans, and running homes for the mentally ill and aged.[11]

Advances in health care continued at a rapid pace throughout the seventeenth century. Although the compound microscope was developed 1590, it wasn't until 1665 that Anton van Leeuwenhoek revealed microscopically the minute structure of living organisms, the existence of red blood corpuscles, and the existence of microorganisms, as well as the presence of sperm in semen.

Treatment for malaria came about when the Countess Ana de Chinchon (fl. 17th c.) introduced to Spain the medicinal powers of Peruvian bark. She had first learned of its curative powers while living in South America with her husband, the Viceroy of Peru. Jesuit Priests explained to her the medicinal use of the bark after having learned of it from the local Indians. When she and her husband returned to Spain, malaria was endemic throughout southern Europe and no treatment was available. News of the new cure spread quickly through Spain, Italy, and finally the rest of Europe. So important was her discovery that the remedy was named Chinchona (quinine) in her honor. "For many years the drug was known to European druggists as `countess's powder'."[12,13]

Edward Sydenham (1624-1689) reintroduced the Hippocratic tradition of bedside observation of the patient. He gave clinical descriptions of malaria, gout, scarlet fever, measles, bronchopneumonia, pleurisy, dysentery, and chorea. He advocated fresh air, diet, and exercise as important factors for healthy living and used simple medications, such as quinine, for treating malaria.

As new treatments surfaced for a variety of illnesses, more emphasis was placed on scientific research. Still, the conditions under which most women delivered their children was still less than adequate in most instances. To improve the practice of midwifery, Elizabeth Cellier (fl. 1680) campaigned vigorously throughout England for training and licensure of all midwives. Statistics she compiled of paranatal, maternal, newborn, and abortion mortality showed that many deaths could have been prevented by the application of proper care. She proposed a hospital that would care for mothers, educate nurses, and find homes for illegitimate children.[14]

Jane Sharp (b. 1620) also recognized the value of a well-trained midwife, but unlike her contemporary Mrs. Cellier, she concentrated her efforts on education. Her book, *The Compleat Midwife Companion* (1671), was the first textbook published in England on the subject and stressed the importance of the study of anatomy by midwives.[15]

Education for women was still unusual, but some were making progress on that front as well. Elena Piscopia (1646-1684) became the first woman of the Renaissance period to receive a doctorate of philosophy. Her academic education at the University of Padua (Italy) covered a wide range of subjects including theology, philosophy, linguistics (she was proficient in seven languages), dialectics, music, and medicine. Her examination in defense of her thesis was conducted in Latin and, because of the large number of people who attended, it was held in Padua Cathedral rather than at the University. She joined the order of Benedictine nuns and continued to teach medicine and mathematics at the University. After her death at age 38 of tuberculosis, a book was published that she had written on mathematics and medicine and several honors were bestowed on her behalf.[16]

By the late 1600's, however, unconventional activities were becoming restricted and witch hunts were becoming common. Although mostly limited to Western Europe, England, and New England, women were especially vulnerable to these accusations. Women who acted as midwives and nurses were often the target of these accusations, since many of their results were unsuccessful. In the seventeenth century alone, 40,000 persons were reported to have been put to death under this guise.

For many, the turmoil created over religious freedom was too much to bear and the promise of a better life prompted thousands to journey to the New World.

One woman who joined the migration to the west was Jeanne Mance (1606-1673), who set out from France to Canada to establish a small hospital, the Hotel-Dieu. She arrived in Montreal in May, 1642 and is considered one of the city's founders. Her task was to build a hospital from funds provided by a wealthy widow in France. By 1645, the Hotel-Dieu, housed in a small cottage, offered 22 beds and a staff of one. Mance served as physician, nurse, administrator, and fund-raiser. In 1649, she returned to France to raise funds, food, clothing, ammunition, and to recruit her own nurses. She remained administrator of the hospital for 30 years, returning to Paris occasionally to raise money and enlist additional help.[17]

The Renaissance was a period of growth and learning. As the era drew to a close new discoveries were offering hope where none had previously existed.

Endnotes Chapter 4

1. Rhodes, *An Outline History of Medicine*, p. 41.

2. Walker, *The Story of Medicine,* p. 79.

3. Christine de Pizan, *The Book of the City of Ladies*, pp. xxi-xxvi.

4. Rhodes, *An Outline History of Medicine*, p. 54.

5. Walker, *The Story of Medicine*, pp. 93-131.

6. *Ibid.*

7. *Ibid.*

8. Marks and Beatty, *Women in White*, pp. 58-59.

9. Chicago, *The Dinner Party*, p. 176.

10. Marks and Beatty, *Women in White*, pp. 57-75.

11. *Ibid.*

12. *Ibid.*

13. Weiser and Arbeiter, *Womanlist*, p. 329.

14. Ogilvie, *Women in Science*, p. 55.

15. *Ibid.*, p. 160.

16. Marks and Beatty, *Women in White*, pp. 57-75.

17. *Ibid.*

Chapter 5

The Age of Enlightenment
1700-1799

The eighteenth century was a period of social awakening and scientific growth. There were minor military skirmishes in the Western world, but the major wars–the American and French Revolutions–occurred toward the end of the century and were products of the vast changes that had taken place. New scientific developments were helping to revolutionize industry as well as the practice of medicine.

The social changes that had occurred were partly a result of the Protestant revolt against the Catholic church. Splinter religious groups formed, such as John Wesley's Methodism, the Pilgrims, the Quakers, and similar groups that incorporated into their religions a concern for the welfare of individuals.

Social change was enhanced by the spread of knowledge to the masses. Travel was becoming easy and accessible to everyone. Migrations of the dissatisfied and adventurous to the Western Hemisphere transmitted new ideas and social philosophies to those establishing communities in the New World.

A new social awareness was demonstrated as hospitals were built with specific social and health-related problems in mind. In London, for example, a maternity hospital was built in 1739, and a foundling hospital for sick and abandoned children was established in 1741. In Edinburgh, a mental institution was founded in 1751, and a school for the deaf in 1760. Public concern for the poor was demonstrated by the founding of the Royal

Humane Society in London in 1777. Similar changes were taking place throughout Europe and the civilized world.

Women had scant influence outside the home during this era. Higher education and professional training were available only to men of the aristocracy. The construction of "lying-in" hospitals designed specifically for childbearing was an indication that more value was placed on women. However, most married women were supposed to be totally involved in child rearing, and were to avoid any pursuits that would diminish their responsibilities to their families.

The medical profession also experienced profound change, building on the developments of the previous era. There was a better understanding of the cause and specific characteristics of disease. Carolus Linneaus' systemic classification of plants suggested similar groupings of diseases. Physiology, a new discipline that incorporated physical sciences, such as chemistry, became recognized as an important factor in the diagnosis and treatment of disease. The central nervous system was recognized as an important factor of disease, and the electrical nature of the nervous impulse was reported. Pathology was organized as a medical specialty when it was discovered that post-mortem findings could be correlated with the clinical picture for a new understanding of disease and treatments. Physicians began to use percussion as a diagnostic tool when it was discovered that physically touching the whole body during an examination gave physicians a new understanding of illness. Previously, diagnosis was based on a recitation of symptoms followed by application of empiric treatments, philosophy, religion, and astronomy.[1]

The benefits of these changes are demonstrated by the population growth during the century, nearly doubling in England, from 5.5 million in 1701 to 9 million in 1800. In 1701, 75% of all children died before age 5 due to infection, malnutrition, and poverty. By 1800, the mortality rate of children under 5 years was only 40%. In spite of all the medical advances, however, serious epidemics ravaged Europe. Smallpox, malaria, and diphtheria spread throughout Europe claiming hundreds of thousands of lives. Influenza, measles, scarlet fever, and typhoid fever were not understood and were ever-present.[2]

One woman though, was intrigued with a technique she observed in Turkey as the wife of the English Ambassador. Lady Mary Wortley Montagu (1689-1763) must have been astonished when she first witnessed the unique process of injecting a small amount of smallpox into the body to obtain a benign immunity against the disease. She agreed to have her children vaccinated against the deadly disease and introduced the concept to the British when she returned home to England.[3]

Progress was indeed being made on many medical fronts. In 1753, the idea was suggested that scurvy was the result of vitamin deficiency and could be prevented by supplemental treatment. Late in the century, the concept of public health was developed. Bloodletting and leeches were still common treatments for many complaints, but a few specific medications such as iron for anemia, were introduced and had gained some acceptance.[4]

However, most of the advances were the result of a better understanding of physical characteristics of disease, since successful specific treatment was still in its early infancy. Physicians could now obtain an organized scientific education at these schools rather than depending on the inadequate uncertainty of the apprentice system. They now served the general population rather than just royalty. Surgery was taken from the hands of the barbers, executioners, and mountebanks, and was given to scientifically trained persons. A licensing system was installed, although superficial criteria for acceptance was still applied. The practice of medicine became a respected, reliable, and remunerative profession.[5]

The use of statistical data was becoming important to the understanding of obstetrics. Marie Jonet-Duges (1730-1797), resident head and manager of the maternity department of the Hotel Dieu in Paris, recognized the significance of statistics and compiled data on 40,000 obstetric cases and wrote several books on childbirth. The innovations which she introduced in the management of labor included repair of the torn perineum, management of placenta praevia, dilatation of the cervix, and version and extraction. She and her husband, an officer of health, studied medicine together. Her daughter, Marie Louis Duges-LaChappelle (1769-1821) worked closely at her side, and, at age 15, she also became a midwife at the Hotel Dieu. She also wrote several books on pregnancy and delivery based on her vast experience at the hospital.[6,7,8]

During the eighteenth century, Austria took over as the leading medical center, due in part to the efforts of Queen Maria Theresa (1719-1780). The eldest daughter of Holy Roman Emperor Charles VI of Brunswick and his wife Queen Elizabeth, Maria Theresa ascended the throne at age 23. Although she was not trained for her responsibilities, she learned quickly and was soon well known for the advancements she instituted. One of her first endeavors as queen was to organize new medical schools and retain renowned teachers and specialists from Holland.

The Viennese clinic became a world-famous teaching center. One of the results of this activity was the opening of a great maternity institution, which by the late 1700's was performing 3,000 deliveries a year. Midwives were carefully trained at the institution, resulting in a mortality rate of 8.4 per 1,000 births whereas in Paris, in 1864, there were 124 maternal deaths from puerperal fever for every 1,000 births. Maria Theresa and her husband, Francis, had 16 children in all, however, only 10 of them lived to adulthood.[9]

Medical education in the eighteenth century was strictly the domain of male students. Dorothea Leporin-Erxleben (1715-1762) was the only female to graduate from medical school in the eighteenth century. She had always shown an interest in medicine as she studied at home with her brother when they were children. When her brother was called for military service, Dorthea petitioned King Frederick II the Great of Prussia to excuse him from duty and to allow them both to attend the University at Halle. The King was quite impressed by her determination and granted her request. She interrupted her studies briefly to marry, but following her husband's death she was left to care for their four children and forced to return to work. Her first book, *Thoughts on Education of the Fair Sex* (1749), was a treatise advocating education for women at the university level.[10]

While women were usually not allowed to study medicine, some intelligent and enthusiastic young women gained invaluable experience from their fathers, brothers, and husbands. Anne Morandi Manzolini (1716-1774) first learned the intricacies of the human body from her husband, an anatomy professor at the University of Bologna. Although she was repulsed by the sight of dead bodies, she would sculpt flawless anatomic wax models for her husband's class lectures. But when he became ill with tuberculosis and they had six children to raise, she was forced to take over the support of the family. She sold many of the models she had created over the years and stepped in for her husband when he was unable to lecture.[11]

> From necessity she started to lecture in her husband's place, dissecting the body and explaining the anatomical relationships of the various parts, and did so with such clarity that she was allowed to take his place, appointed Lecturer in her own name after his death and elected Professor of Anatomy in 1766.[12]

She continued to lecture for years following the death of her husband. She was invited to speak in Britain, where she became a member of the Royal Society, and in Russia, where she was elected to the Russian Royal Scientific Society.[13]

The late 1700's saw remarkable growth in technology as well. The Industrial Revolution began to have an impact on society soon after James Watt invented the steam engine in 1765.

Advances were also being made in the field of obstetrics. In 1797, Martha Mears (fl. 1790's) wrote and published *Candid Advice to the Fair Sex on the Subject of Pregnancy*, a practical guide to gynecology and obstetrics but it did not dwell on unusual problems of pregnancy. She stressed that pregnancy was a normal process and not an illness. The importance of a healthy ancestry was stressed. She urged readers to practice good hygiene during pregnancy and decried interfering in a normal delivery even in an attempt to hasten the process. She did approve of the use of the newly introduced forceps, however. Uterine hemorrhage, the contagious nature of puerperal infection and treatment of swollen legs were all discussed in her manual as well as the dangers of artificial abortion. Methods of predicting delivery dates and the unreliability of astrology were also discussed. She urged patients to receive smallpox vaccinations. She gave rules for midwives, recommending that they call a skillful physician when complications were observed.[14,15]

Toward the end of the century, however, the rights of women were becoming a serious pursuit. A landmark book, *The Vindication of the Rights of Woman*, by Mary Wollstonecraft (1759-1791), was published in 1792. The book obtained wide distribution and addressed the state of the middle-class woman. She advocated serious education of women as a means of strengthening the family unit. "How many women thus waste life away the prey of discontent, who might have practiced as physicians, regulated a farm, managed a shop, and stood erect, supported by their own industry."[16] She was denied an education and educated herself at home. She argued that equal employment for single women was a right. An earlier piece, *Thoughts on Education of Daughters* (1786), argued that if women were to contribute to the development of society, then they would have to be properly prepared with a solid education.[17]

In 1793, in France, women were given civil rights, rights in marriage, property, and education, but denied political rights. The fight for women's rights was making progress, or so they thought until Napoleon gained power in 1799.

Endnotes Chapter 5

1. Walker, *The Story of Medicine*, pp. 132-171.

2. *Ibid.*

3. Lois Decker O'Neill, ed., *The Women's Book of World Records and Achievements*, pp. 197-198.

4. Charles Singer and E. Ashworth Underwood, *A Short History of Medicine*, pp. 187-204.

5. Walker, *The Story of Medicine*, pp. 132-171.

6. Marks and Beatty, *Women in White*, p. 67.

7. *Ibid.*

8. Ogilvie, *Women in Science,* p. 116.

9. Edward Crankshaw, *Maria Theresa*, pp. 42-67.

10. Ogilvie, *Women in Science*, p. 82.

11. Susan Raven and Alison Weir, *Women of Achievement*, p. 234.

12. Macksey and Macksey, *The Book of Women's Achievements*, p. 144.

13. Uglow, ed., *The International Dictionary of Women's Biography*, p. 304.

14. Kate Campbell Hurd Mead, *A History of Women in Medicine from the Earliest Times to the Beginning of the Nineteenth Century*, pp. 472-474.

15. Chicago, *The Dinner Party*, p. 176.

16. Mary Wollstonecraft, *The Vindication of the Rights of Woman,* in *History of Ideas on Women*, Rosemary Agonito, p. 157.

17. Uglow, ed., The International Dictionary of Women's Biography, p. 504.

Chapter 6

Industrial, Social, and Scientific Revolutions
1800-1849

The only major war to mar the period between 1800 and 1850 was the
Napoleonic war which culminated in Napoleon Bonaparte's defeat at
Waterloo in 1815. England, under the rule of Queen Victoria (1837-1901)
entered into an imperialistic period and expanded into Afghanistan, India,
China, South Africa, and Australia.

The Industrial Revolution continued to make its mark and contribute
great scientific advances. A growing social awareness developed, medicine
as a science was expanding, the need for public health was appreciated, and
women were finally emerging from the home, in most cases to provide
charitable services.

The social problems spawned by industrialization continued to grow.
Working class individuals of all ages were putting in 12- to 13-hour days,
under dangerous and unsanitary conditions, for inadequate wages. The
extreme poverty was contrasted with the great wealth of a few manufacturers,
mine owners, and landed gentry. Living conditions improved for the wealthy
because of the new industrialization, but grew deplorable for the poor. Gas
street lighting was one of the socioscientific benefits, but sanitation remained
a problem for all but the upper classes, and water supplies often were impure.

With the advent of passenger trains and the steamboat the public could
travel and move to new locations. Mass migrations, whether to new
countries, or from rural areas to cities, occurred and created fertile soil for

the influence of social writers, such as Charles Dickens. The introduction of the telegraph improved communications, and mail service stimulated the dissemination of ideas between the people of Europe and the Americas.

Government in England and the United States now saw the importance of influencing the social structure. In 1819, laws were passed to limit the working hours of juveniles to 12 hours per day. Women and children were prohibited from working underground in 1842, and working hours were further reduced to 10 hours in 1847. Trade unions were legalized in 1824, and in 1832, the upper middle class was enfranchised in England. Slavery was abolished in the British Empire in 1833, and the Spanish Inquisition was suppressed in 1834. With this growing social responsibility came greater concern for public health. In 1815, the Apothecaries Act specifically forbade the practice of medicine by unqualified doctors. In 1838, the Registration Act was passed requiring registration of all births, deaths, and marriages. A Sanitary Commission was founded in 1839. By 1848, the Public Health Act was established, as was a General Board of Health.

Augmenting this new social awareness was a virtual explosion of scientific knowledge, particularly in the medical and health fields. Scientific knowledge, which was based on the developments of the previous generation, resulted in a new understanding of the human body and of disease. Epidemics continued, however, since the causes of specific diseases, and the means to control them, were still unknown.

Great medical centers were established, and information was shared between nations and the various scientific disciplines. Most could easily travel to meeting places to exchange knowledge and experiences. Improved communication within the medical community was aided by journals, such as *The Lancet,* first published in 1823. The British Association for the Advancement of Science was founded in 1831, and the British Medical Association was established in 1832. Scientists in all European countries were involved in better understanding the interrelationship of medicine, physics, chemistry, physiology, biology, microscopy, and anatomy.

Microscopic study and autopsies correlated clinical observations and pathology, and the ability to identify specific diseases emerged. Diseases of the kidney, lymphatic system, heart, the arthritides, Parkinsonism, the various diarrheas, and exophthalmic goiter all were gaining greater understanding. New comprehension of the cell, the nucleus, the ovum, the effect of nervous tension on the stomach, anatomy of the brain and spinal nerves all brought the medical picture into greater focus.

Surgery did not advance as quickly as the other fields and was limited by ignorance of antisepsis, and an absence of anesthesia. However, in spite of these limitations, the first successful ovarectomy was performed in 1809, and an operation to correct an aneurysm was completed in 1841. Surgery had to be performed quickly, since the use of nitrous oxide and ether as anesthetics was not introduced until 1844.[1]

Still, these advancements were made by men, because the idea that "the woman's place is in the home," dominated the upper and middle classes. Most working-class women, however, did not have the luxury of staying home. In order to support an ever-growing family, the women and children had to find work in factories and mines.

One woman, however, defied society's strict rules for women and successfully masqueraded as a man during her entire professional career as a prominent surgeon in the British Army. James Barry (1793-1865) was recognized as the first female physician in England only after her death revealed her true sex. Although not much is known of her early life, it is believed she was born Miranda Stuart, who was raised by her aunt and her "Uncle Barry." Following the death of her uncle, she was sent to live with General Francisco Miranda who tutored her, and encouraged her interest in science. Some suggest that he decided that her future would be assured if she pursued a career in medicine disguised as a man.[2] Donning a wig and three-inch heels he introduced her as a young man of age 10. Although she was actually in her teens, her feminine features prompted her to conceal her true age when she enrolled at the University of Edinburgh in 1809. She usually kept to herself and while most thought she was odd, few questioned her gender, and no one doubted her skill.

Shortly after her graduation at age 20, the young doctor studied surgery, and then entered the British Medical Service as a surgeon. She was an able leader and quick to defend her masculine honor. She fought bravely at the Battle of Waterloo and was considered a good shot. When instigated, it is said she was quick to challenge an annoyer to a duel. In 1816, she was posted at a garrison in Capetown, South Africa, where she performed at least one successful Caesarean section, the first reported such operation in Africa, and the second such operation in modern history in which both the mother and child survived.[3]

By 1827, she had attained the rank of Surgeon Major which gave her the advantage of private living quarters which helped hide her true identity. She made controversial and strict administrative decisions about health care, sanitary conditions, and diet for the sick. She introduced female nursing care for female patients in a civilian hospital in St. Helena, and advocated separate living quarters for the married officers. She was uncompromising in maintaining the highest standards of the medical profession, and she prohibited the administration of potent drugs by anyone other than qualified physicians or licensed apothecaries.

During a tour of duty as principal military officer in Malta, she suffered a bout of yellow fever. Near death, she ruled that she was to have no visitors and, if she died, she was to be buried immediately, with her clothes on. She didn't die, however, and eventually took on a new assignment as Inspector General of Hospitals in Corfu. She served in a similar position in Canada, where she altered the soldiers' diet, improved the water and drainage systems, and established the first separate quarters for married soldiers and their wives.

Dr. Barry retired from the Army on half-pay in 1859, following a siege of infl uenza and eventually died in 1865. During her terminal illness and following her death, the physician, out of deference to her rank, did not examine her. It was the embalmer who reported her gender to the military. Because of this discovery, she was not permitted to be buried in the military burial ground.[4]

Women's status did not improve much during the early half of the nineteenth century, but some women felt a need to speak out on issues that were often ignored, and they set out to change deplorable human conditions. Dorthea Dix (1802-1887) was a teacher who was so shocked by conditions she saw at Middlesex House of Corrections that she devoted most of her career to reforming the prison system and mental institutions.

The eldest of three children, Dorthea was sent by her sickly mother and alcoholic father to live with her grandmother at age 12. She realized early on that in order for her to support herself adequately, she would have to be well educated and took on the task of educating herself. She read voraciously and dreamed of one day starting her own school. By age 14, she had accomplished her goal and within 5 years she had opened several schools and, in 1821, she established a free school for poor children above her grandmother's stable. She was totally dedicated in her role as a teacher and worked long hours to make sure the children had a good education. Her hard work took its toll, however, and by 1824, she was completely exhausted and suffering from tuberculosis. Her doctors insisted she take a long rest, but she worried about how she would support herself. Not long after that she accepted a position as a governess which gave her the opportunity to rest, but also supported her financially. When she was back on her feet, she opened a new school in Boston, in 1831. Her success was again short-lived for soon after the new school opened, the tuberculosis returned. Her doctors adamantly insisted she rest this time. She took their advice and travelled to Italy and England.

She returned to Cambridge in 1837, and was told that volunteers were needed to teach Sunday School to the female inmates of The Middledsex House of Corrections. It was here she discovered that mentally ill patients were housed in worse conditions than the criminals. Horrified by the conditions she witnessed, she immediately began her campaign for reforms. She spent the next 18 months inspecting all the jails and almshouses in Massachusetts. She took her data to the state legislature demanding change. "I come as an advocate of the helpless, forgotten insane and idiotic men and women, of beings sunk to a condition from which the most unconcerned would start with real horror." She described the inmates as "confined. . . .in cages, closets, cellars, stalls, pens: chained naked, beaten with rods, and lashed into obedience."[5]

As a result of these efforts, Massachusetts passed a law providing appropriate funds for improving the care of the mentally ill. She then moved her crusade on to other states. She covered over 3,000 miles between 1837 and 1847, examining prisons and mental institutions. She inspired reform in

15 states and played a direct role in founding 32 mental hospitals. Through her inspiration the number of mental hospitals in the United States increased from 13 in 1843 to 123 in 1880.[6]

As women made strides in health reform, others stressed the importance of education for women. Catherine Beecher (1800-1878) was a teacher who also lectured and wrote about the value of higher education for women. She maintained that women should be taught methods of problem solving, and that domestic science should be taught by women rather than men. Through education, she believed, women could develop independence and self-respect. The home was to be the woman's sphere of responsibility, according to Beecher. All of her writings and reforms were geared to an indignant sense of disparity between women's true role and her actual condition as an exploited factory worker, a worn, incompetent housewife, or a corseted and indolent creature of wealth.[7]

Although education was her primary concern, she was more successful and influential as an author and lecturer than as a school operator. She opened the Hartford Female Academy in 1824 with her 13-year-old sister, Harriet Beecher Stowe (1811-1896) acting as her assistant. But, the school eventually failed from lack of funds. Between 1832 and 1837, she ran the Western Female Academy in Cincinnati, which also closed for financial reasons, and because of her own poor health.

Although Harriet is probably best known for her book, Uncle Tom's Cabin (1852), she and Catherine co-authored 19 books on domestic science. In 1929, Catherine wrote a pamphlet proposing that schools be endowed and that teachers should be assigned to limited fields of teaching. She travelled, lectured, wrote articles and books on household management as well as encouraged higher education for women.[8]

In 1843, Catherine published *Treatise on Domestic Economy* which covered every aspect of domestic activity and, in 1846, she published *Miss Beecher's Domestic Recipe Book* which described basic cooking techniques and offered recipes. This pseudoscientific approach to cooking was novel at the time. She also devoted time to organizing women's groups toward teaching as a profession.

In 1847, together with William Stroud, she formed The Board of National Popular Education which trained many school teachers and in 1852, she organized the American Women's Educational Association, whose goal was to educate girls in the "West" as teachers and homemakers. And while she advocated education for women, she was also an active antisuffragist, believing that women should be educated to become better wives and mothers who will be able to manage the home scientifically.[9]

By then it might have been too late: the feminist movement was in full swing. In 1848, under the under the guidance of Elizabeth Cady Stanton and Susan B. Anthony, women's social stature was changing and the drive to obtain women's rights was well under way.

Endnotes Chapter 6

1. Rhodes, *An Outline History of Medicine*, pp. 91-115.

2. Joan Marlow, *The Great Women*, p. 51.

3. Elizabeth Longford, *Eminent Victorian Women*, pp. 232-354.

4. *Ibid.*, pp. 238-246.

5. Marlow, *The Great Women*, pp. 52-57.

6. *Ibid.*

7. Edward T. and Janet W. James, *Notable American Women, 1607-1950, a Biographical Dictionary*, vol. I, pp. 122-125.

8. *Ibid.*

9. *Ibid.*

Chapter 7

War and Social Conscience
1850-1874

As the feminist movement began to pick up some support in the mid-nineteenth century, new emphasis was being placed on social and health problems in the Western world. However, this was a particularly bloody period in world history with three major wars dominating attention. During the Crimean War (1853-1856) the Russians and Turks battled for Crimea, a peninsula extending into the Black Sea, and eventually brought England and France into the conflict. In the United States, the Civil War (1861-1864) threatened to permanently divide the North and South over economic, social, and constitutional issues. And, in Europe, the Franco-Prussian War (1870-1871) was waged to unite the German states under Prussian control. But it was also because of the wars that women began to break down the barriers they had previously been unable to budge. Women were needed to care for the wounded, and many bravely accepted the challenge by offering their services to the war efforts.

On the home front, new developments in medicine prompted a greater emphasis on public health. In England, in 1853, vaccinations against smallpox became mandatory. In 1855, following a devastating cholera epidemic, a modern sewer system was established and improved health conditions were demonstrated by the fact that their population doubled between 1815 and 1871–in spite of the fact that 424,000 British citizens emigrated to the United States..[1]

Those who left Britain often were looking for a better life or to make a fortu ne in any of a number of trades now available in the United States. Samuel Blackwell was a successful sugar refiner and Liberal dissenter who sought to enhance his fortune by moving his family to the United States in 1832. He wanted the best for his nine children and insisted they have all have good educations. Most of his children were high achievers, but Elizabeth (1821-1910) showed a strong interest in the sciences. Still, women were restricted from practicing medicine, so she took a teaching position in the Carolinas. The urge to practice medicine was strong, however, and she continued to pursue a medical education. After being rejected by 29 medical schools, she was finally accepted at one, Geneva Medical School in New York. She must have been delighted that she had finally won the respect of the school's administration, and devastated to learn that her application, which had been put before the students to decide, was accepted more as a joke than for her ability to become a physician. She persevered in spite of the "joke" and graduated in 1849, as the first woman to receive a medical degree in the United States. After receiving her medical degree, Dr. Blackwell was accepted as a student midwife at La Materité in Paris, but soon after her arrival, a severe eye infection, which later resulted in blindness in one eye, forced her to relinquish her position at the hospital. By 1850, Dr. Blackwell had accepted a position in the wards of St. Bartholomew's Hospital in London.[2]

She returned to the United States in 1851, and tried to establish a medical practice. When it became apparent that no one would rent space to the young, female doctor, she ultimately decided to purchase a one-room house she converted to a dispensary, and, in 1854, opened her own office in the slums district of New York. Dedicated to treating the poor, she treated over 200 indigent women in her first year alone. While her practice grew, providing a much-needed service to those in the neighborhood, Dr. Blackwell devoted much of her time and effort to delivering health lectures to the community. *The Laws of Life with Special References to Physical Education of Girls,* attempted to teach women about their own anatomy and physiology a message she considered important.[3]

Her desire to help women motivated her to establish a hospital conducted by women for the treatment of indigent women and children of New York, as well as to train women as physicians and nurses. In 1857, with the help of her sister Emily Blackwell (1826-1910) and their friend Marie Zakrewska (1829-1902) as resident physician and general manager, she opened the New York Infirmary for Women and Children. The infirmary, which had obtained a state charter, provided women with practical experience. The small institution was primitive with the dispensary on the first floor, a six-bed ward on the second, a maternity ward on the third floor, and sleeping quarters for five medical students in the attic. Here, the women cared for 3,000 patients during their first year of operation. Some of the patients were treated for free, others paid a small three-dollar fee. Once the infirmary was on solid footing, however, Elizabeth left the hospital and returned to Europe to advance opportunities for women in medicine.[4]

When she returned to England in 1859, she ran into her old friend Florence Nightingale (1820-1910), whom she had met while studying in Paris. Florence was a nursing student at the time, and the two became good friends. Both young women had come from similar backgrounds, and both shared a desire to help the sick and wounded. After Elizabeth returned to the United States, Florence left for Crimea. Florence was determined to break the age-old prejudice against women in the army and establish nursing as a reputable profession. In 1854, she organized a party of 38 nurses for duty in the Crimean War at the Hospital at Scuturi in Turkey. "She was appalled by the grim conditions and inadequate supplies at the Scuturi hospital. The barracks were dirty and dilapidated; there were no bandages and a dearth of bedding and food; and anarchy reigned among the hospital staff. The situation cried out for a capable coordinator."[5] And, Florence Nightingale was just the leader they needed. Until now attention had been focused solely on corrective measures but she shifted the emphasis to preventive care as she introduced new hygienic standards into military hospitals so that within a year the death rate among patients had dropped from 42% to 2.2%. She had a similar experience in Baclava in 1855, where her sanitary reforms led to a decrease in typhus, cholera, and dysentery.[6]

Now she was back in London to appeal to Queen Victoria to convene a commission to investigate health policies in the Army, and to institute badly needed reforms. She won her health care reforms and because of her efforts was the first woman to be awarded the Order of Merit by Queen Victoria. During this period, she served as adviser to the first district nursing service and organized the appointment of women health commissioners. She was a strong believer in research and devoted a good portion of her energy to compiling statistics. In 1857, she wrote *Notes on Matters Affecting the Health, Efficiency, and Hospital Administration of the British Army* and, based on her experiences as a body of data to prove the necessity of a new system, the entire structure of the War Office was reorganized over the next five years. Her skill as a statistician enabled her election to the Royal Statistical Society, and for her to be granted an honorary membership to the American Statistical Society.

In gratitude for her work in Crimea, the British public raised £44,000 to endow the Nightingale School to train nurses at St. Thomas Hospital in London. It was the first fully endowed school of nursing and combined technical ability with professionalism and established standards in nursing ultimately raising it from its former menial status. It was her missionary purpose in nursing that enabled her to bring her methods of nursing and hygiene into many hospitals, workhouse infirmaries, and district nursing areas throughout England and Europe. Her expertise led to her instrumental role as the architect of a massive Indian Sanitary Commission. Throughout the latter part of her career she was an adviser and an international consultant on military and civilian nursing, hospital planning and management, and on public health[7]

Public health continued to generate interest and all scientific disciplines were contributing to medical advances. The invention of the ophthalmoscope and laryngoscope made it possible for physicians to see inside the human body. Louis Pasteur established the validity of the germ theory of disease. Meanwhile, surgeon Joseph Lister introduced antisepsis into the operating room.[8]

Science was also introducing controversial issues at an alarming rate. Charles Darwin published *Origin of the Species*, in 1859, which explained his theory of evolution. Clerk Maxwell published his paper *Treatise on Electricity and Magnetism.* Pasteur was making progress in his experiments with pasteurization, and ultimately developed the process for pasteurizing wine. In medicine, physiologist Claude Bernard discovered the mechanisms of digestion, metabolism of glycogen, and vasomotor activity. Meanwhile, Gregor Johann Mendel published the results of his experiments on heredity.[9]

Controversy surrounding issues of heredity and roots led to an even greater social and moral dilemma in the United States–the issue of slavery. While many other underlying issues, such as state's unity, actually led to the Civil War, it was abolitionist leader John Brown's seizure of Harpers Ferry, West Virginia that initiated the bloodiest war in United States history.

The citizens of the United States had never seen anything like it. Thousands of soldiers were wounded and horribly disfigured. Clara Barton (1821-1912), was working in the Washington Patent Office when the war broke out. She was deeply touched by the war, and began to organize a distribution effort for food and medical supplies. "The Angel of the Battlefield" carried her supplies directly to the front lines in mule trains and refused any assistance from the Army. She believed that she could sidestep much of the red tape if she acted independently.[10]

Others participated too. Dorthea Dix became involved with the military health set-up, and worked tirelessly for reform. She organized the first secular nursing in the United States with the development of the Army Nursing Corps. In 1861, she was appointed superintendent of the army nurses in the Union Army. But, she was known for her imperious character and was often controversial, and therefore, often ineffective. Her fund-raising activities were extraordinary, for she raised more money for charitable purposes than had anyone else before her.[11]

One woman refused to bow to tradition and culture and marched onto the battlefield in men's trousers. Mary Walker, MD (1832-1919) was the first woman surgeon in the United States Army, and the only woman to receive the Congressional Medal of Honor.

After Dr. Walker's graduation from Syracuse Medical College, she and her husband, Dr. Albert Miller, opened a joint practice in New York State. In addition to her busy practice, she lectured and campaigned for a relaxation of women's dress. "Corsets are like coffins," she proclaimed as she refused to conform to the style of the day. When the war began, she volunteered to work in tent hospitals in Virginia. "She took risks crossing Confederate lines to attend civilians and was imprisoned for four months in 1864."[12]

Following the war, Dr. Walker lectured in favor of prohibition, anti-smoking, revised marriage and divorce laws, labor laws, freedom of religion, hospitals for morally unfortunate women, women's rights, as well as social and political equality for women. She was often socially ostracized because of her unconventional proposals. "Always an unconventional dresser, after the war she wore a man's full evening dress and silk hat for her many lectures on women's rights."[13]

The Reconstruction that followed the Civil War was a time of prosperity and growth for the United States and the expansion to the West was in full swing. "A symbol of the North's triumph as a nation-builder came with the driving of the final spike of the transcontinental Union Pacific railroad in 1869."[14]

A new social conscience was developing in the United States and Europe. The Civil War freed the slaves; France instituted an old-age pension; tenement reform was established in London and, in 1865, the Salvation Army opened its doors. Education of the less fortunate became important, and the Working Man's College was founded in London. Women proceeded to make strides in education, science, and medicine. The end of the Civil War also marked the slow beginning of change for black women when Rebecca Lee (fl. 1860's) became the first to receive a medical degree from New England Female Medical College.[15]

Technology was moving at a rapid pace. The first transatlantic cable provided communication between the old world and the new. In New England, the Massachusetts Institute of Technology was founded after demonstrating the need for specialized scientific training in addition to conventional scholarly education. And, it was technology that freed women from domestic drudgery with inventions, such as the electric washing machine, sewing machine, and vacuum cleaner. Women were finally being accepted in new coeducational institutions as women's rights were being forcibly presented to the public under the leadership of Elizabeth Cady Stanton, Lucy Stone, and Susan B. Anthony.

Meanwhile, in Europe, the women's rights movement was picking up momentum. Medicine and the arts were fields in which women could work independently so more were starting to enter health-related fields. But marriage and family were still considered to be the things to which most proper young ladies aspired. And, once married, women were supposed to stay at home and certainly not have a career. One woman, however, was determined to prove that a married woman could succeed in her profession without neglecting her family. Elizabeth Garrett Anderson (1836-1917) first learned of the accomplishments of Elizabeth Blackwell in 1859 and was determined to follow in her footsteps. She had always been a bright student and was often disappointed in her female teachers' lack of understanding of science. Her father had always been a proponent of equal education for both boys and girls, and he had seen that his daughters had the best educations possible. After attending one of Dr. Blackwell's lectures on the need of women to pursue medical educations, Elizabeth made her decision to become a doctor.

Medical schools were not as receptive to the idea of female students and she was forced to rely on medical tutors for her early education. She entered school as a surgical nurse at Middlesex Hospital in London, in order to gain access to dissections and operations, fully intending to attend medical school, but without letting anyone at the school know her plan. She was eventually accepted as an unofficial medical student but after some time was denied access to lectures because the men insisted she was a distraction. Between 1863 and 1865, she studied for her Apothecaries' license. She continued to forge new ground for women and, again following the inspiration of Elizabeth Blackwell, she opened the St. Mary's Dispensary for Women in 1866. This institution was also staffed by women and was located in a poor area of London, called Marleybone. During one year of operation, the hospital saw 3,000 patients–mostly because of a cholera epidemic. Dr. Anderson, however, displayed a particular empathy to the prostitutes in the area and was deeply concerned with their problems. She was outspoken in her efforts to obtain basic civil rights for women and children.

Finally, it was announced that London University had reversed its charter and would now permit women to earn their degrees. It was a tremendous struggle for her to complete her studies, but she prevailed. She continued her education and in 1870, she passed the six examinations needed to obtain her medical degree from the Sorbonne in Paris, thus becoming the first woman in France to receive an MD in modern times. Still, because of her gender, she was barred from a hospital appointment in England, and was forced to set up a private practice. She was now more determined than ever to improve the situation for women in medicine. She was instrumental in establishing the London School of Medicine for Women where she served as president, dean, and lecturer.[16]

The issue of married women holding medical degrees was a difficult one in the late 1800's. Mary Putnam Jacobi, MD (1842-1906) demonstrated the capacity of a married woman to meet the demands of a successful medical practice and provided a stimulus for raising the standards of medical education for women. By example, she demonstrated the fallacy that women were biologically, emotionally, and intellectually incapable of practicing medicine. Both explicitly, and by implication, she challenged her female colleagues and students to aspire to her own high standards of professional achievement.

She was born in London, but moved to the United States with her family when she was age 5. Her father, publisher George Palmer Putnam, was supportive of her desire to study medicine, but he also stressed the importance of remaining "feminine." She graduated from the New York College of Pharmacy in 1863, and went on to earn her medical degree from the Female Medical College of Pennsylvania. In 1868, she was the first woman to be admitted to Ecole de Médecine in Paris. Upon her return to the United States in 1872, she organized the Association of Medical Education of Women, which later became the Women's Medical Association of New York. In addition to her organizational endeavors and clinical lectures, she was professor of Materia Medica and Therapeutics at Women's Medical College of New York Infirmary for Women and Children. It was her interest in the conditions of poor women and children that prompted her to organize the National Consumer's League which worked to abolish sweatshops. She published more than 100 papers on pathology, neurology, pediatrics, physiology, and medical education. An article, "The Question of Rest for Women During Menstruation," earned her the Boylston Prize from Harvard University. She had a particular interest in what would now be referred to as "psychosomatic medicine," especially as it related to women. And, she took a strong interest in environmental conditions that contributed to illness. She combined a successful home life and private practice with a wide range of hospital, educational, and professional responsibilities.[17]

But the struggle to be treated as an equal was far from won. "As the numbers of women physicians increased, new labels were used to denigrate them. In the late 1800s they were labeled witches; later they were called abortionists."[18]   But the feminist movement was behind them as women became an important force in the medical fields.

Endnotes Chapter 7

1. Singer and Underwood, *A Short History of Medicine*, pp. 204-220.

2. Uglow, ed., *The International Dictionary of Women's Biography*, pp. 60-61.

3. James and James, *Notable American Women, 1607-1950, a Biographical Dictionary*, pp. 161-164.

4. *Ibid.*, pp. 164-167.

5. Marlow, *The Great Women*, p. 82.

6. *Ibid.*

7. Uglow, ed., *The International Dictionary of Women's Biography*, pp. 343-344.

8. Rhodes, *An Outline History of Medicine*, pp. 91-106.

9. *Ibid.*

10. Raven and Weir, *Women of Achievement*, p. 220.

11. Uglow, ed., *The International Dictionary of Women's Biography*, p. 147.

12. *Ibid.*, pp. 485-486.

13. Raven and Weir, *Women of Achievement*, p. 245.

14. Burns and Ralph, *et al.*, *World Civilizations*, p. 916.

15. Chicago, *The Dinner Party*, p. 191.

16. Jo Manton, *Elizabeth Garrett Anderson*, pp. 222-354.

17. Marks and Beatty, *Women in White*, pp. 122-128.

18. Perihan Aral Rosenthal and Judith Eaton, "Women MDs in America: 100 Years of Progress and Backlash," *Journal of the American Medical Women's Association*, p. 130.

Chapter 8

Growth and Expansion
1875-1899

The years preceding the turn of the century were relatively free of conflict as the United States continued a tremendous rebuilding and expansion phase. Clara Barton continued to make headlines and gain international attention as she strongly urged the United States to adopt an American Red Cross. Having seen the Red Cross movement expand throughout Europe, she lobbied the International Committee of the Red Cross for the United States to be included in the eleven-nation Geneva Treaty.[1] In 1881, the American Association of the Red Cross was established with the intent to aid the suffering–whether a result of natural or man-made disaster–until suffering no longer existed.

While humanitarian efforts were capturing the public's attention, so, too, were the latest gadgets, conveniences, and scientific developments. Telephones were cropping up in private homes. Transportation was growing at a phenomenal rate as railroad networks developed and steamboats were able to transport food and people to remote areas of the world. In London, an underground subway was available and the streets were lit by electricity.

However, conditions for women hoping to study medicine did not change dramatically. Progress was being made by Sophia Jex-Blake (1840-1912) who opened the London School of Medicine for Women in 1874, but even she had not been able to receive a medical degree and was forced to continue her studies in Switzerland. Only after her graduation from the University of Bern in 1877 was she permitted to practice medicine in England. Although it took her over 12 years to earn the right to call herself a physician, she was persistent has she had always been. As the daughter of aristocrats, Sophia had decided early on that she would do more than accept the leisurely lifestyle of many of her contemporaries. She became a tutor at Queen's College in London, but her father insisted she not accept payment for her services. It wasn't until she began teaching in Germany that she actually received compensation for her efforts. On a trip to the United States, Sophia volunteered at New England College for Women and Children. It was an experience that changed her life–she now was determined to be a doctor. She applied to several medical schools in the United States and was rejected by all but the Women's Medical College of New York Infirmary who accepted her as their first female student. Shortly after her admittance to the College, her father died and she was forced to return to England. Unable to complete her studies in the United States, Sophia was accepted with four other women to the University of Edinburgh Medical School in 1869. The women were rejected and ridiculed by the other students and faculty members, who ultimately prevented the women from graduating. This was the final insult and Sophia sued the University for refusing her a degree. She lost her case and felt the only way to overcome the devastation was to establish a medical school for women.

"Sophia's personality was forceful, and a clash of views with Elizabeth Garrett Anderson caused her to leave the London School and return to Edinburgh in 1878."[2] There, she founded what would later become the Edinburgh Hospital for Women and Children, and another medical school for women. She continued to advocate woman's admittance to men's medical schools and eventually ended her campaign when for lack of need both women's schools were forced to close in the 1890's.[3]

Women who studied the sciences were considered a rare breed, but there were a few standouts. One remarkable example is Ellen Swallow Richards (1842-1911) who so impressed the administration at Massachusetts Institute of Technology (MIT) that in 1870 she became the first woman admitted to a scientific college. She was admitted as a special student on the condition that she not pay for her classes; therefore, she would not be recognized as an official student. She had already earned a Bachelor of Science degree from

Vassar College at the time she entered the institute, and was such a brilliant student that she was awarded a BS degree from MIT in 1873–the same year she was awarded a master's degree from Vassar. In addition to her studies, she taught a chemistry course to teachers and students at a girl's school in Boston. She continued her graduate studies at MIT but, by the time she was eligible for her PhD in 1875, the Institute had not yet awarded a doctorate in chemistry to any student and administrators were reluctant to award the first one to a woman. Ellen was forced to wait until a man had received his degree before she was granted her doctorate degree.

Degree or not, she remained active at the Institute where she established and headed the women's lab, which provided training in chemical analysis, industrial chemistry, mineralogy, and biology. She also advised women on health and finances. Through her teaching, research, publications, and public involvements, Ellen played a major role in the growth of ecology, dietetics, and home economics. She was determined to bring the standards and procedures of the scientific laboratory into the American home. Standards were beginning to be applied to foodstuffs and in 1878-1889 she conducted widespread investigations of the adulteration of staple groceries for the Massachusetts State Board of Health. Her courage, determination, ability, and success ultimately influenced school administrators to accept women students into the regular course of study in 1882. Administrators also responded by allowing her to set up the first chemistry laboratory for the study of sanitation to train the world's first public health engineers. She continued as an instructor in the department for the next 27 years. During her tenure she prepared pamphlets for the US Department of Agriculture on the nutritive value of foods, and was the first to make a comprehensive study of the scientific basis of nutrition. A leader in dietetics and home economics as a profession, she revolutionized the art of cooking by quantifying measurements and standardizing ingredients. "She witnessed radical improvements in the American diet and sanitation system; she opened doors for the female population in science education; she elevated the status and eased the burden of housekeeping, making women more productive and happier."[4]

This was an exciting time for housewives who were being liberated from housekeeping duties with the introduction of the electric vacuum cleaner, iron, and sewing machines. Also, frozen and canned foods were appearing on the market for the first time, and the food industry was offering more options to consumers than any other time in history. Housewives now had more choices to provide a healthy diet for their families, which also led to more confusion: How could women provide a nutritious meal for a large family on a tight budget? The answer came at an exhibit of the World's Colombian Exposition in Chicago, where Ellen presented visitors to the "Rumford Kitchen" with a healthy, low-cost meal. That idea led to the New England Kitchen in Boston. "In 1984, the New England Kitchen became the purveyor of lunches to the Boston public schools, and soon other schools and hospitals were employing Ellen as a dietary consultant."[5]

Scientific applications to housekeeping responsibilities also interested Ellen Richards enough to organize a department of Home Economics at Simmons College in Boston. In 1899, she brought together a group interested in the betterment of the home, and, at a meeting in Lake Placid, NY, worked out courses of study to make up the discipline of Home Economics. She continued well into the early part of the twentieth century to develop the American Home Economics Association and establish the *Journal of Home Economics*.[6]

As interest in food management and safety became more widespread, the need for dietetics to become recognized as a specific science in the field of medicine and health maintenance was becoming more apparent. Sarah Tyson Rorer (1849-1937) demonstrated the need for a scientific approach to healthy eating as an early pioneer in dietetics. A graduate of East Aurora Academy, she attended lectures on pharmacology, physiology, anatomy, and biochemistry at the University of Pennsylvania and Women's Medical College of Pennsylvania. In 1879, she enrolled in The New Century Cooking School and in 1882 she opened her own school, The Philadelphia Cooking School, where students trained to become hospital dietitians. She taught cooking, dietetics, as well as biology, chemistry, physics, and anatomy. She included marketing, the mechanics of food preparation, and the chemical principles of food in her curriculum. She was an early advocate of the use of margarine over butter, she stressed the dangers of overeating, and she recommended fruits instead of heavy desserts. Perhaps her greatest challenge as well as most rewarding experience came, however, when a prominent physician asked her to supervise the opening of a diet kitchen where he and other physicians could refer their patients for dietary guidance. Finally, it seemed, the health aspects of diet were being accepted by the medical profession.[7]

The medical profession was not so quick to embrace the issue of birth control for women. "By the 1860s, birth control was practiced by both the middle and upper classes and the working poor. The methods of, reasons for, and attitudes about birth control, however, were vastly different among the social classes."[8] While birth control methods were widely used, however, many publicly condemned any form of contraception with the most vocal opponents being physicians.[9] At a small surgical center in Holland, one female physician, who had been providing free surgery for the poor, began advocating use of a diaphragm to prevent pregnancy in her patients. Aletta Jacobs (1849-1929) was a unique woman in Holland when she became the first female in her country to receive a medical degree. Soon after she began to offer her services to the poor, she realized that the information she was offering was too vital to be limited to her small practice. In 1882, she opened the world's first birth control clinic in Amsterdam and made it available to her patients. In addition to her pioneering work in birth control, she was involved in other campaigns to improve the position of women in society. She often spoke of the need to reduce working hours, introducing legislation to increase safety at work, provide education about venereal disease, abolish regulated prostitution, as well as reforms in the penal system and marriage laws.[10,11]

Gradually, women were gaining acceptance to postgraduate education, although it was always an uphill struggle. Mary Elizabeth Garrett (1854-1915) had a profound influence on medical education in the United States–especially the medical education of women. Her father was the president of B&O Railroad and, although she did not have a college education herself, Mary was able to tap the resources of her wealthy friends and relatives for support. In 1885, she, together with three friends, established Bryn Mawr

School for Girls. She was also involved in the new medical school being established at Johns Hopkins. Before it's completion, the school desperately needed over $300,000 to continue construction. She agreed to provide the money and, in 1889, stepped in with the much-needed funds. Her generous support for what would become a leading institution in medical education, was contingent upon the stipulations that (1) women be admitted and rewarded on the same basis as men, and (2) that the school always be a graduate school, requiring that entrants only come from accredited colleges. The courses required for admission were to include biology, chemistry, physics, and a reading knowledge of French and German.[12]

The field of medicine itself was undergoing drastic changes at this time as scientific developments vastly improved its effectiveness. Bacteriology had become an essential tool of diagnosis since specific causes of some diseases could now be visualized. Robert Koch developed a method of staining and culturing bacteria. He identified specific organisms, such as those causing tuberculosis, anthrax, and cholera. He also outlined a procedure for proving the causative organism in given disease. The malaria parasite had also been identified as had filiaria.

Protection against disease was now becoming a reality. Antitoxin to modify diphtheria infection and vaccine injection against hydrophobia were developed. Anna Wessels Williams (1863-1954) was a bacteriologist who, in 1894, isolated a strain of Diphtheria Bacillus which possessed an unusual capability of generating toxin. From this strain a vaccine was prepared for active immunization of babies against diphtheria. During the next two years she investigated bacteriology of streptococcal and pneumococcal infections. In 1896, she was invited to the Pasteur Institute in Paris and while there provided a culture of rabies vaccine. In 1898, she returned to the United States and was able to provide sufficient vaccine to begin large-scale rabies vaccine production. She contributed greatly to the understanding of infectious diseases, and actively championed preventive immunization of children against contagious disease.[13]

More emphasis was now being placed on the patient as a whole individual and nursing had, by now, become a highly regarded and valued profession for women. Rose Hawthorne Lathrop (1851-1926), daughter of author Nathaniel

Hawthorne, was interested in helping those who were suffering from incurable cancer. With only a three-month practical nursing course, in 1888 she rented a tenement in the slums of New York where she established a nursing home for those with terminal cancer and whose families did not have enough money to pay for care. Considered a forerunner of the Hospice movement, the success of her initial attempts to set up nursing facilities led her to the purchase, in 1889, of a three-story brick building which she founded as St. Rose's Free Home for Incurable Cancer. Patients would be seen on an outpatient basis, and the home was dependent on donations for support. Gradually, she expanded her facilities as she developed a group of volunteer helpers until she had five additional facilities in the suburbs of New York. In addition to the nursing homes, she founded the Servants of Relief for Incurable Cancer branch of the Dominican Order of Sisters.[14]

As more people immigrated to the United States, and those in rural areas flocked to the city looking for jobs, conditions in cities continued to deteriorate. The gap widened between the living conditions of the haves and have-nots with laborers working under deplorable conditions. All these situations combined to aggravate health and social problems.

Social problems were being attacked aggressively, at least in the larger cities. Jane Addams (1860-1935) recognized the need for an institution to serve the growing immigrant population of Chicago. Hull House, the first settlement house in the United States, was established in 1889 to help immigrant workers and their families adjust to life in their new country. Hull House provided educational opportunities as well as cultural and recreational activities. "By 1893, Hull House was a center with some 40 clubs, a day-care program, a gymnasium, a playground, a dispensary, and a cooperative boarding house for working girls. Each week, some 2,000 Chicagoans entered its doors to partake of the course offerings and to socialize with their neighbors."[15] Jane had always had a desire to help people and had early on expressed a desire to become a doctor. She graduated as president and valedictorian of her class at Rockford (Illinois) Seminary and went on to study medicine at Women's Medical College in Philadelphia. Her father's sudden death and her chronic spinal problems forced her to give up her dreams of becoming a doctor and she returned to

Illinois. On a trip to Europe, she visited a renowned settlement house in London called Toynbee Hall. She encouraged a travelling companion, Ellen Starr, to join her in her new venture and together they founded Hull House. As time went on, Jane saw the need to go beyond the role of the traditional settlement house. She wanted to see real changes made in the neighborhoods. In 1895, she presented to state and national legislatures, a detailed study of living conditions in Chicago's 19th ward. *Hull House Maps and Papers* gave documented evidence that reforms were necessary to relieve conditions in the slums. As a result, the first factory inspection act was passed in Illinois as well as reforms in juvenile court law and mother's pension law. "Hull House became a target for political reactionaries and defenders of the status quo, who viewed the center as a hotbed of social and political agitation."[16]

Among the many volunteers at Hull House was Florence Kelley (1859-1932), a lawyer and social reformer dedicated to seeing that laws be passed protecting working women and children. She had experienced the personal devastation of being turned down for law school because she was a woman. After receiving her education in Europe, she joined the radical Socialist Party and married a party member. She divorced her husband shortly after her return to the United States, and moved with her three children to Hull House. "There was at that time no statistical information on Chicago industrial conditions, and Mrs. Florence Kelley. . . .suggested to the Illinois State Bureau of Labor that they investigate the sweating system in Chicago with its attendant child labor," wrote Jane Addams.[17] Mrs. Kelley lead the investigation which resulted in the passage of legislation to regulate sanitary conditions in factories and set a minimum age limit of 14 years for employment in sweatshops. As the first woman factory inspector, Florence initiated legislation to limit a working day to 8 hours. She continued her fight for social justice after leaving Hull House and joining the Henry Street Settlement in New York. She was involved with the National Consumer's League and was a founding member of the National Association for the Advancement of Colored People (NAACP).[18]

Hull House continued to be a strong force in the community and a leader in bringing issues of poverty to the forefront of the nation's attention.

Endnotes Chapter 8

1. Alden Whitman, ed., *American Reformers*, p. 59.

2. Uglow, ed., *The International Dictionary of Women's Biography*, pp. 244-245.

3. *Ibid.*

4. Marlow, *The Great Women*, pp. 129-133.

5. *Ibid.*, p. 133.

6. Margaret W. Rossiter, *Women Scientists in America*, pp. 68-69.

7. E. Neige Toddhunter, "Biographical Notes from a History of Nutrition: Sarah Tyson Rorer," *Journal of the American Dietetic Association*, 1963; 1:75.

8. Teri Perse, "The Birth Control Movement in England and the United States: the First 100 years," *Journal of the American Medical Women's Association*, 40; 4:119-122.

9. *Ibid.*

10. Uglow, ed., *The International Dictionary of Women's Biography*, p. 241.

11. Emily Taft Douglas, *Margaret Sanger: Pioneer of the Future*, p. 83.

12. Thomas B. Turner, "Women in Medicine, a Historic Perspective," *Journal of the American Medical Women's Association*, 36; 2:34.

13. Rossiter, *Women Scientists in America*, pp. 68-69.

14. James and James, *Notable American Women, 1607-1950, a Biographical Dictionary*, pp. 372-374.

15. Marlow, *The Great Women*, pp. 174-175.

16. *Ibid.*, pp. 172-175.

17. Jane Addams, *Twenty Years at Hull House*, p. 201.

18. Uglow, ed., *The International Dictionary of Women's Biography*, p. 255.

Chapter 9

The Twentieth Century Begins
1900-1924

As the world entered the twentieth century, political, social, scientific, and medical changs were sweeping the world at breakneck speed. Industry was bursting with new technology. The expansion that followed the Civil War in the United States, as well as in Europe, was continuing.

Construction of the Panama Canal began in the early years of the new century. The work was grueling and attempts to create a sea-level canal between the Atlantic and Pacific oceans often ended in frustration. In addition to having to cut through solid rock to build the canal, workers were constantly besieged with epidemics of malaria and yellow fever.

Yellow fever had been a serious problem throughout South America and the Caribbean. Researchers, however, had an idea: if the disease was spread by mosquito, then it could be controlled. Volunteers were needed to test the hypothesis and one young army nurse, stationed at an army camp in Cuba promptly signed up. Clara Maass (1876-1901) submitted to the test which meant being bitten by an infected mosquito and, within a short time, began to experience symptoms of the disease. It was a mild case and she quickly recovered. Still anxious to continue the study, she allowed herself to again undergo another test. This infection was far more serious than her previous illness, however, and she died at age 25.[1] It was obvious, though, that the disease was indeed transmitted by the insect and steps were taken to drain the swamps to control disease. "At the outset of construction, thousands of workers fell sick every year. The incidence of sickness was cut to about seven per 1,000 employees by 1914, the year the waterway opened."[2]

New inventions and ideas were being touted by highly trained engineers as well as backyard mechanics–and no idea was too outrageous. Even the age-old challenge of flight was tried and tested in fields, farmyards, and off any elevation imaginable. In all parts of the United States and Europe people tinkered with their flying machines, but it was Wilbur and Orville Wright who actually recorded the first flight in 1903. Not only did this monumental feat give way to the beginning of a new industry, it also symbolized a new spirit of industrial growth. While airplanes were being tested and improved, automobiles were revolutionizing transportation. In 1908, Henry Ford introduced the Model-T, which was the first affordable automobile produced on an assembly line. Mass production of goods and services changed the way business, industry, government, and society worked. The face of the country was changing and everyone wanted in on it.

Along with increased prosperity also came a downside. Now, disease related to the new industries was creating a problem and a new field of study was developed–industrial and occupational disease. Alice Hamilton, MD (1869-1970) was a pioneer in the field of industrial illness and initiated many laws to protect workers in dangerous occupations. After receiving her medical degree from the University of Michigan, and doing postgraduate work in Europe, she accepted a position at the Women's Medical College at Northwestern and moved to Chicago in 1897. She was able to pursue her interest in bacteriology and pathology while she also did social service work as a resident of Hull House.

She performed a variety of tasks at the settlement house including operating a clinic for young mothers and babies, while she continued her lectures at the college.[3] In 1902, when a typhoid epidemic spread throughout Chicago, she suggested that the epidemic was probably spread by the flies surrounding inadequate sewage disposal.[4] She continued to investigate threats to the public and initiated campaigns against tuberculosis, cocaine, and a new area of concern, industrial disease.[5] In 1910, she was appointed to head the Occupational Disease Commission where she was the first to study the effects of lead on workers of various industries. Her department studied 304 businesses and discovered 77 lead-using processes that exposed employees to poisoning. She identified 578 certain victims of the disease, thus marking the first time that modern laboratory techniques were combined with field study.[6] Dr. Hamilton became the country's leading authority on lead poisoning and her studies documented the high mortality and morbidity ratio, first in lead and, later, during World War I, she uncovered the effects of poisons used in producing munitions.

She continued her crusade to improve health conditions in the workplace until she was appointed assistant professor of industrial medicine at Harvard Medical School and the first woman professor at the school. "Hamilton's move to Harvard coincided with a new phase of industrial medicine in the United States. After the war, the danger of industrial diseases increased markedly, keeping pace with the nation's rapid economic expansion."[7] When she was appointed to the same position at the newly formed Harvard School of Public Health (1922) she was hired with the stipulations that she (1) would not be admitted to the Harvard Faculty Club, (2) could not participate in the academic procession at graduation and, (3) she would not be eligible for faculty seats at the football games. She suffered the injustice and spent her entire career there until her retirement as assistant professor emeritus. Her work for reforms in dangerous occupations prompted her to publicize the effects of these new toxins in her book, *Industrial Poisons in the United States* (1925). The book established her as a leading authority on the subject and prompted the Surgeon General to call a national conference on the effects of tetraethylene lead in 1925, and radium in 1928.[8]

During her years at Hull House, Alice Hamilton frequently consulted with her close friend and co-worker, Julia Lathrop (1858-1932). Julia was a social reformer interested in the issues of juvenile delinquency and the plight of the mentally ill. After her arrival at Hull House in 1890, she became active on the Illinois Board of Charities. She lobbied for reforms in relief programs for children and the mentally ill. In 1912, she was appointed the first director of the Federal Children's Bureau where she instituted many landmark studies which resulted in significant reforms. Under her direction, the Bureau appealed for uniform birth registration procedures and later studied maternal and infant mortality, nutrition data, juvenile delinquency, the juvenile court system, illegitimacy, and mental disorders. The bureau also surveyed existing laws regarding child labor and mother's pensions. In addition to their lobbying efforts to institute new legislation, they also were responsible for enforcing child labor laws.[9]

Infant mortality was an issue that also was brought to the forefront during this period. One of the vocal advocates of children's health was Sara Josephine Baker, MD, PhD (1873-1945). As assistant to the New York City Health Commissioner, she founded the Health Department's Division of Child Hygiene, designed to demonstrate the value of well-baby care and the prevention of disease in children. She had a flair for public relations, and early on developed innovative techniques for bringing current medical knowledge to the poor and disadvantaged. She, along with 30 nurses, canvassed an entire district of New York which was made up of mostly Italian immigrants. She and her assistants would teach the young mothers some basic principles of child care, breast feeding, as well as proper bathing and dressing techniques. "By the end of the hot summer, infant deaths in the district had dropped 1,200 from the previous year, while the mortality rate in other areas showed no significant change."[10] As a result, she was able to start the first tax-supported agency designed to improve children's health. In her role as director of the agency, she distributed pamphlets on good hygiene, provided training for midwives and established a clinic for children.

> As an administrator Dr. Baker was characterized by a pragmatic willingness to improvise and by an interest in even minor improvements. A new foolproof container which she helped design for eye medications used at birth aided in reducing infant blindness, and her patterns for sensible and healthful baby clothes were adapted for commercial use by the McCall Pattern Company.[11]

In 1909 she helped found the American Child Health Association and in 1911 she organized the Babies' Welfare Association (which later became the Children's Welfare Federation of New York), whose goal was to coordinate the work of private agencies. An accomplished author and lecturer, she once agreed to lecture at New York University's Bellevue Medical School on the condition that they grant her acceptance into the new public health course. In 1917, she became their first woman Doctorate of Public Health.[12]

While some progress was being made in children's services little help was available for the severely handicapped. In fact, had it not been for the determination, courage, and strength shown by Helen Keller (1880-1968), many of those who suffer handicaps would still be relegated to a life of confinement and dependency. Helen's struggles as a deaf and blind child were first brought to the public's attention when she published her first book, *The Story of My Life* (1902) which detailed her education under her tutor and governess Anne Sullivan Macy (1866-1936). Miss Sullivan arrived at the Keller home to find Helen almost a wild animal, unable to communicate with anyone. Theirs was a special relationship based on love and discipline. Anne Sullivan had been recommended to Helen's parents by Alexander Graham Bell. He had seen the young Helen who was left unable to see or hear following an illness when she was an infant. Anne Sullivan, who was herself visually impaired, was able to successfully teach Helen sign language to communicate with the outside world. Together, they demonstrated to the world the growth potential of a seriously handicapped individual when provided the proper stimulus and emotional support.

Eventually, Helen proved to be such a bright student that she was taught an oral language, and was able to graduate from Radcliffe College in 1904. *The Story of My Life*, created such widespread national awareness of the problems of the handicapped that she was invited to lecture extensively throughout the country. Her lectures were popular and created a public awareness of the problems faced by handicapped individuals. As her schedule permitted, Helen and her co-author John Macy, cotinued to write books, and participate in civil and women's rights movements as well as initiatives to abolish child labor and capital punishment. In 1924, she became involved with the American Federation for the Blind and eventually began to lobby in Washington for legislation to assist the blind and provide them with a much-needed federally funded reading service. She also worked to include the blind in the Social Security Act.[13,14]

Helping the less fortunate was a common interest among the middle- and upper-class women of the early 1900's. Women's clubs sprang up to provide charitable services to the poor and handicapped. Emily Bissell (1861-1948) was a social welfare worker from Delaware who conceived and organized the Nationwide Christmas Seal Campaign to raise money for the fight against tuberculosis. Having always been active in social and civic organizations, Emily had organized recreational programs and sponsored the first free kindergarten in the United States. She was also involved in the organization of the Delaware Chapter of the American Red Cross. Through the Red Cross, she was able to initiate a program similar to the one she had heard was taking place in Denmark of selling special Christmas stamps to raise money. In its first year Emily's Christmas Seal Campaign raised $3,000. The following year, the first national campaign netted almost $135,000.[15]

Organizations such as the National Tuberculosis Association were established to focus research dollars on finding new medical and scientific advances. As science became more sophisticated and medicine absorbed scientific developments, the preservation of health, and the treatment of disease improved. There was a growing awareness of intangible factors in body chemistry. Vitamins and amino acids were identified and recognized as necessary for good health. The functions of ductless glands were discovered and the relationship of insulin to diabetes was recognized. Finally, aggressive treatments could be offered for the usually fatal disease diabetes.

Catalysts and enzymes were found to be involved in body functions and blood types were identified. Allergy, and its relation to histamine and anaphylaxis provided new relief to allergy suffers. And the role of the subconscious and the conditioned reflex were now identified as physiologic factors in body activity. Research was also advancing in areas of genetics when the existence of chromosomes was suggested, and in some circles a link between cancer and the environment was being discussed. Important new preventive measures and treatments were introduced: mosquito control to prevent yellow fever; salvorsan for syphilis; thyroxin for thyroid deficiency; raw liver for pernicious anemia; heparin to control blood clots; and insulin for diabetes.

Alice Evans' (1881-1975) most widely recognized contribution was her discovery and confirmation of the etiology of Brucellosis in humans. She established the relationship of Bangs Disease in cattle to Brucellosis in humans. An equally, or perhaps more, important contribution was the identification of the sources of bacterial contamination of milk and her insistence that raw milk presented a danger to human health which could be overcome by pasteurization. Such a claim could not be made, however, without inspiring the hostility of the dairy farmers and the suspicion of physicians. She started her career with the Dairy Division Bureau of Animal Industry at the US Department of Agriculture. She held several positions within the department and quickly learned the ins and outs of working in a political system. Eventually, her warnings took hold and pasteurization of milk sold to the public resulted in improved control of many diseases such as tuberculosis, streptococcal infections, and other bacterial infections.[16]

The ways food impacted health were gaining more attention in political and social circles now. Alice Lakey (1857-1935) was a community leader who ably assisted Harvey Wiley in the Pure Food Movement in the United States. They first met when he, as chief of the chemistry division of the Department of Agriculture, was invited to speak about "food adulteration" to the ladies of the Cranford Village (New Jersey) Improvement Association. Alice was immediately impressed with his message and promptly joined his crusade. She enlisted the New Jersey Women's Association to petition Congress to pass pure food legislation, but she wasn't content to stop there. She enlisted the assistance of the General Federation of Women's Clubs and pressed the National Consumer's League into forming an investigation committee. She used dramatic exhibits of impure and adulterated food to drive home her point. After the Federal Food and Drug Act requiring labelling of ingredients on all prepackaged food and drugs passed in 1906, she went on to organize the New York Milk Committee, designed to promote a healthful milk supply for New York City residents.[17]

A new understanding was developing about how knowledge and education could lead to life-saving therapies and cures. In the laboratory, scientists were exploring new theories of energy, matter, and the nature of man. X-rays were developed and the structure of the atom realized. In Paris, Pierre (1859-1906) and Marie (1867-1934) Curie spent years in their lab trying to unlock the mysteries of radium. The Curies were brilliant scientists who in 1903, after years of research, won a Nobel Prize in physics for determining the atomic weight of radium. They worked well together and maintained a professional working relationship while enjoying a happy home life as well. Neither could have foreseen the tragedy that would befall them three years later when Pierre was killed in a serious accident. Marie felt compelled to finish the work the two had started, and eventually became a respected scientist in her own right.

She was born in Poland as Manya (Marie) Sklodovska, to a professor of physics and a well-educated aristocratic mother. She could read by the time she was four and, after suffering a childhood filled with personal tragedies, she decided on a career as a governess in order to save enough money for her sister to become a doctor. Her sister married a doctor in Paris and soon sent for Marie to live with them. Upon arriving in Paris, Marie enrolled in physics classes at the Sorbonne. It was here she met and, after a brief courtship, married Pierre Curie. She had always dreamed of returning to Poland, but stayed instead with Pierre in France. She began her work on radium in 1897, but it wasn't until winning the Nobel Prize that she gained international celebrity for her research efforts. After Pierre's death, she took over his lectures at the University of Paris and continued the radium research. She oversaw the development of the Institute of Radium between 1909 and 1914, and won a second Nobel Prize for her work in radiation therapy in 1911.

> When war came, Marie Curie invented an X-ray apparatus to be attached to ambulances known as `little Curies.' Marie Curie herself drove one of the `little Curies' for the duration of the war, as well as training 150 French recruits, drawn from all socio-economic classes, as radiological technicians.[18]

Science was for the first time having a true impact on population as more understanding was acquired on the origins and treatment of certain diseases. Science had learned how to control many fatal diseases and infant mortality was decreasing. Overpopulation, however, was becoming a concern by the early twentieth century. The one person who, perhaps, had the greatest effect on the world's population was Margaret Sanger (1879-1966) who risked her own personal health and safety to campaign for a woman's right to choose motherhood. She was a married, mother of two who became bored with her suburban housewife role and returned to work as a visiting nurse in New York City. In addition, she was an active Socialist and wrote a column on women's health for the Socialist paper called, "What Every Girl Should Know." When her column dealt with the issue of gonorrhea, she was accused of pandering obscene material.

Shortly after this she responded to an emergency call from a man whose wife was dying of complications of a backstreet abortion. The wife's ultimate death prompted Margaret to try to see that every woman in the country have access to accurate birth control information. After a trip to Europe to see how they were handling birth control issues, she began to publish *The Woman Rebel*, a monthly magazine dealing with a variety of information for women. She again faced federal charges, but on the day she was supposed to defend herself in court, she left the country and went back to Europe. Before her departure to England, she had published a book, *Family Limitations*, on how to use various methods of contraception. "When Margaret Sanger landed on British soil, she received word that 10,000 copies of *Family Limitations* were in the mails. This bible of the birth control movement was eventually to sell 10 million copies and was translated into 13 languages."[19]

When she returned to the United States in 1916, she and her sister opened the country's first birth control clinic. "That day, 140 women stood patiently in line from dawn until the closing hours of the clinic. Each day, the clinic was jammed by women who had read circulars in English, Italian, and Yiddish inviting them to obtain `information [on birth control] from trained nurses at 46 Amboy St'."[20] Despite the clinic's success, however, Margaret was again arrested under "public nuisance" laws. Undaunted, she continued to write and lecture, and with the support of her second husband, Noah Slee, she was able to fund many research projects. Margaret Sanger endured arrest, public ridicule, and humiliation before she was finally able to see her organization gain legitimacy when the president of the American College of Obstetricians and Gynecologists joined the Sanger Clinic's board and the American Medical Association endorsed contraception as a valid medical procedure.

While Margaret Sanger was mired in controversy in the United States, Marie Carmichael Stopes, PhD (1880-1958) was creating just as much of a stir in London when she and her husband opened the first birth control clinic there in 1921. She was a successful botanist when she published *Married Love* in 1918, which was the first sex manual to focus on women's pleasure. That same year she published *Wise Parenthood* which dealt more specifically with contraceptive measures. Both sold millions of copies and were translated into 13 languages. In 1921, the birth control clinic opened to offer free advice to disadvantaged women who could not afford the services of a physician. "Needless to say the medical profession was hostile. Stope's lack of a medical degree was frequently jeered at–and the Roman Catholics attacked her even more fiercely."[21] One of her critics went too far, however, when he claimed setting up the clinic was a "serious crime," and she countered by suing him for libel. The trial brought national attention to Stope's cause and, although she lost her case, she was able to spread her message to the millions of women who needed her practical information.

Women were beginning to reap the benefits of the feminist movement as they obtained suffrage in Austria in 1907, in England in 1918, and in the United States in 1920. Coeducational colleges and women's colleges made education available that was on par with men's educations. Life as a single woman was now feasible and, in some cases, preferable to life with men.

Women rebelled against the common stereotypes perpetrated by men when they realized that women were not too frail to compete in the classroom or the laboratory. Leta S. Hollingsworth (1886-1939) was a psychologist and educator who exploded the myth of male intellectual superiority after being denied a teaching position in the public schools when administrators learned she was married. This devastating experience affected her deeply. She became an avowed feminist and was determined to break the stereotypical differences that existed between men and women. Using carefully controlled studies, she studied the traits of various age groups of men and women. She included newborns, college-age students, and women during their menstrual cycle. She found no evidence of feminine impairment and challenged the popular teaching of male superiority of the time.

> There was thus by 1916, a growing and increasingly vocal scientific feminism that used anthropological and especially psychological data to undermine and discredit traditionally antifeminist social science, usually on the grounds of inadequate logic or methodology.[22]

Women were still having difficulty gaining acceptance into graduate schools and usually did not have easy access to financial aid. Their biggest hurdle came, however, in the workplace where they still were not eligible for positions of power commensurate with their training. One area in which they were permitted to expand and apply scientific principles was in the application of home- and family-related developments.

A revolution was occurring in the home itself. Many time- and energy-consuming chores of the home had been eased with such labor-saving devices as electric irons, vacuum cleaners, washing machines, and toasters. Mass factory production of clothes took one more activity away from the modern housewife. As household chores eased, the woman's role changed dramatically. Her clothing was simplified and less restrictive. Hemlines which touched the floor in 1900 had risen to just above the knees in 1920. Families were learning to eat foods that were canned outside the home.

As the principals of refrigeration became better understood more emphasis was placed on frozen food. An early pioneer in food research was Mary Engle Pennington (1872-1952) who went to work for the US Department of Agriculture (USDA) soon after graduating from the University of Pennsylvania. She played an instrumental role in the passage of the Pure Food and Drug Act (1906) and was later asked to head the Food Research Laboratory. While there she completed research on the correct temperatures for properly freezing food and was an expert in the safe temperature for refrigerated food in freight cars.[23]

The medical community and consumers were starting to realize the benefits of a healthy diet. Frances Stern (1873-1947) was a pioneer in dietetics who gained recognition through her founding of The Boston Dispensary a Food Clinic in 1918. The first institution of its kind, the Food Clinic trained young dietetic interns, students of home economics, nursing, and social work. Students who were interested in medicine, dentistry, and public health service also took her nutrition courses. Perhaps her greatest contribution was her development of a dietary program for outpatients designed to enhance medical treatment.[24]

One disease that couldn't be treated with diet alone, however, was scarlet fever. The crippling disease, which killed 25% of its victims, was rampant throughout history. Gladys Dick (1881-1963) and her husband George, were both physicians and microbiologists who collaborated on kidney pathochemistry. They took a particular interest in the study of scarlet fever after their only son died of the disease in 1914. They persevered, however, and in 1923, Gladys and George proved that scarlet fever was caused by hemolytic streptococcus. In 1924, they discovered that the strep bacteria released a toxin that caused the rash of the disease, leading the way for a skin test to determine susceptibility to the disease. Finally, they developed the method for active immunization against the disease by the use of toxin/antitoxin.[25]

The "roaring 20's" were a time of increasing free expression and knowledge. Women were sharing in the new freedoms available to them. Education, it seemed, was finally being recognized as the key to independence.

Endnotes Chapter 9

1. O'Neill, ed., *The Women's Book of World Records and Achievements*, p. 232.

2. "Panama Canal," *Encyclopedia Americana*, p. 348.

3. Barbara Sicherman, *Alice Hamilton, A Life in Letters*, p. 119.

4. *Ibid.*, p. 145.

5. *Ibid.*, p. 146.

6. *Ibid.*, pp. 157-158.

7. *Ibid.*, pp. 238-239.

8. Sicherman, *Notable American Women, The Modern Period*, p. 305.

9. Uglow, ed., *The International Dictionary of Women's Biography*, pp. 270-271.

10. James and James, *Notable American Women, 1607-1950, a Biographical Dictionary*, p. 85.

11. *Ibid.*

12. *Ibid.*, p. 86.

13. Uglow, ed., *The International Dictionary of Women's Biography*, p. 255.

14. Sicherman, *Notable American Women, The Modern Period*, pp. 389-393.

15. James and James, *Notable American Women, 1607-1950, a Biographical Dictionary*, p. 153.

16. O'Neill, ed., *The Women's Book of World Records and Achievements*, p.216.

17. James and James, *Notable American Women, 1620-1950, a Biographical Dictionary*, vol. II, p. 360.

18. Marlow, *The Great Women*, p. 202.

19. *Ibid.*, pp. 242-243.

20. *Ibid.*

21. Raven and Weir, *Women of Achievement*, p. 244.

22. Rossiter, *Women Scientists in America*, p. 115.

23. *Ibid.*, p. 219.

24. Mary Pfaffman, "Frances Stern," *Journal of the American Dietetic Association*, pp. 110-111.

25. Sicherman, *Notable American Women, The Modern Period*, pp. 191-192.

Chapter 10

Economic Depression through the Atomic Age
1925-1949

Dramatic events gripped the years between 1925 and 1950, which was an era dominated by economic disaster, war, and tremendous scientific breakthroughs. Exploration into new areas of the world captivated western civilization with news of Roald Amundsen's dirigible flight over the North Pole in 1926 and Admiral Richard Byrd's explorations of the South Pole. Charles Lindbergh made headlines all over the world when he became the first to make a nonstop transatlantic flight from New York to Paris in 1927.

Women were making some strides in a number of fields and, by 1925, had appeared to have won the education battle in the Western world. But, they were still limited in their power to utilize their new-found educations. Women demanded and were gaining the right to have a voice in political matters. In 1925, women in England were finally given the right to vote. In areas previously dominated by men, women were showing off their abilities to compete in sports and pursue less feminine activities such as golf and tennis. In 1926, Gertrude Ederle tested her strength and skill when she became the first woman to swim the English Channel.

Women's entrance into the fields of medicine and science was still resisted, but they were making advances, particularly in health-related fields. Women were slowly being accepted as capable researchers. By 1925, Florence Rena Sabin, MD (1871-1953) had made such an important contribution to medical research that she had earned the right to her appointment as first woman to join the National Academy of Science. As a medical student at Johns Hopkins, she was attracted to the growing field of anatomy. A paper she wrote while still in school, *An Atlas of the Medulla and Mid-brain,* was published in 1901 as a medical text while she still was completing her internship. Following graduation, she became the first woman medical faculty member at Johns Hopkins when she took a position as assistant in the anatomy department. She concentrated on studying the lymphatic system where she challenged the prevalent theory on the origins of the lymphatic system and popularized a form of nontoxic staining to study live cells. Perhaps her greatest contribution was her 25-year career as a teacher. "A student in 1909 described her lectures as `very rapidly spoken' because `she was so enthusiastic in trying to correlate the scientific and medical aspect of anatomy'." When Dr. Sabin left Johns Hopkins in 1925 to join the Rockefeller Institute in New York as its first woman member, she turned her attention to similar research projects.[1,2]

Many contributions were made in the fields of child care and nutrition–traditional areas of interest and aptitude for women. Contributions were also being made by women in neurology, psychiatry, bacteriology, pathology, medicine, and the application of science in the home.

Child-rearing was even taking on a scientific approach as more young mothers learned new aspects of child development and psychology. The needs and feelings of children were just beginning to be understood as researchers began to accept the notion that children were more than "miniature adults." Melanie Klein, MD (1882-1960) was an Austrian psychiatrist who was one of the first to engage in child analysis. In 1926, after receiving training as a psychoanalyst in Budapest and Berlin, Dr. Klein settled in London to pursue her interest in applying psychoanalytic techniques to young children. She evolved a system of play therapy to supplement the usual psychoanalytic procedures. By providing the child with small toys representing family members, she could elicit the child's subconscious feelings. Her intuitive perceptions about child behaviors elicited by these new techniques led her to discover what goes on in a child's subconscious mind, even as young as two years of age.[3]

A different, more pragmatic technique was employed by Anna Freud (b. 1895), the youngest daughter of psychoanalyst Sigmund Freud. She practiced psychoanalysis and expanded on the work of her father until they were forced in 1938 to flee their native Austria for England to escape religious persecution. In England, "she aimed to create a developmental profile of a child, rather than laying too much stress on obscure pre-verbal periods."[4] She also emphasized the importance of the parent-child relationship.

The attitudes children carried into adulthood was the primary focus of Karen Horney, MD (1885-1952) who was the first psychoanalyst to challenge Freud's theories of female "penis envy." She insisted that women were, in fact, more envious of men's superiority in a society that treated women as second-class citizens. Her father was a firm believer that women should not pursue education, but she persisted and enrolled at the University of Frieburg (Germany). In 1919, she joined the Berlin Psychoanalytic Clinic (later the Psychoanalytic Institute) where she became a popular speaker on the subject of female sexuality. In 1932, she moved to the United States where she eventually joined the New York Psychoanalytic Institute. She still met resistance to her theories and resigned in 1940. The following year she founded the Association for the Advancement of Psychoanalysis.[5]

As the responsibilities of the modern housewife became less physically demanding, her role became less well defined. Electric refrigerators and automatic washers were common in most homes, while packaged and precooked meals became standard fare in many homes. Virginia Woolf (1882-1941) wrote a disturbing essay, *A Room of One's Own* (1929), in which she maintained that it was impossible for women to be truly creative when required to be productive within the confines of the usual chaotic home. The problems women faced in raising a family were compounded by harsh economic factors of the early 1930's. The great depression, which started with the stock market crash of 1929, spawned a need to apply scientific principals to household management.

Medicine, on the other hand seemed to have limitless potential. A specific chemical to treat each specific disease was a realistic goal. Deficiency disease could be avoided and treated as the various vitamins and trace minerals were identified and synthesized. After the development of penicillin, a variety of antibiotics were developed in rapid succession. Diseases such as syphilis, gonorrhea, pneumonia, streptococcal infections could be treated with drugs such as streptomycin, Aureomycin, Chloromycetin, and others. It appeared that there was a potential for ridding the world of disease.

Science was becoming highly regarded and medicine was known for its conservative approach to new ideas and treatments. In Australia, a nursing sister encountered years of ridicule and professional rejection when she challenged the conventional theories for treating poliomyelitis. Elizabeth Kenney (1886-1952) theorized that muscle spasm constantly accompanies the pain of poliomyelitis and, therefore, is a factor that must be addressed in treatment. Her treatments involved simple exercises, hot baths and hydrotherapy directed toward the muscle spasm, rather than the common use of splints to support the opposing weakened muscles.

Sister Kenney had seen first hand the suffering of polio victims. It was out of desperation that, as a young bush nurse in the Australian outback, she first applied hot towels to the legs of a young patient who was writhing in pain. The treatment calmed her down immediately, allowing the child to sleep. As word spread of her unconventional yet miraculous treatments, more patients sought her assistance, so that by 1913 she had established a small cottage hospital for polio patients in which the parents served as aides. The hospital continued to operate until she was ridiculed by the Medical Society of Brisbane. Nevertheless, in 1933, during a polio epidemic in Queensland, she opened a new clinic to treat polio patients.[6] The clinic in Townsville gained public recognition and was given government support. Her critics denounced her theories on the basis that she was a nurse, not a doctor, and that she came from rural Australia rather than a well-recognized medical establishment. However, she used her determination and persistence to focus the public's efforts on finding a cure or preventive vaccine for the disease. Her forcefulness of character and popularity with the public led to the establishment, in 1935, of a royal commission to examine her ideas. In 1937 she published a book, *Infantile Paralysis and Cerebral Diplegia–Methods Used for Restoration of Function*, explaining her treatment methods. The Commission issued an unfavorable report of her methods the following year, but the Australian government allowed parents to decide between her treatment methods and conventional treatments. It wasn't until decades later that her theories became accepted in the medical community. But, the many patients she served never asked for endorsement from a conventional medical establishment to know her methods were correct.[7]

Women's presence in the lab was still scarce, but the few who did conduct experiments were providing essential new evidence in the war against life-threatening diseases. Maud Caroline Slye, MD (1869-1964), was a pathologist who did extensive experiments on mice which proved that contagion is not a primary factor in the transmission of cancer and that the susceptibility is inherited. She began her breeding experiments with mice, studying the relationship of heredity and cancer while a graduate assistant in the Biology department at University of Chicago. In 1913, she presented her first paper on cancer research which involved 5,000 mice of which 298 spontaneously developed cancer. Her conclusion was that cancer was inherited, not transmitted by contagion. She continued her research and interest into the causes of cancer and, in 1936, presented evidence that more than one gene is involved in cancer. She maintained that there were actually two genetic factors involved; one determined the type of cancer; the other determined the location. While this theory was oversimplified, her extensive and meticulous studies helped to clearly establish the role heredity plays in determining susceptibility to cancer.[8]

The mid-1930's saw an explosion of interest in the research areas of biochemistry and physiology. The same year that Maud Slye presented her cancer theories, biochemists Gerty Cori, MD (1896-1957) and her husband Carl, demonstrated the characteristics of the breakdown of glycogen. Their discovery was one of a number of breakthroughs they were involved in throughout their careers. The couple met while students at the Medical School of the German University of Prague, and following their graduation as medical doctors in 1920, both went to work at the Karolinen Children's Hospital in Vienna. Both had a strong desire to work in medical research and, in 1922, Carl accepted a position at the New York State Institute for the Study of Malignant Diseases. When Gerty joined her husband in the United States she was offered a position as assistant pathologist. In 1925, she was named assistant biochemist and was allowed to collaborate with her husband on research projects. They pursued their interest in carbohydrate metabolism as well as cancer research. By 1931, the Coris had decided their research was going beyond the realm of interest to the institute and Carl accepted a new position at Washington University School of Medicine in St. Louis. "University rules at the time prohibited faculty appointment of two members of the same family, but Gerty Cori was given a research position at a token salary in the same department." Here they continued their research into metabolism and their work "became a focal point for all workers interested in carbohydrate metabolism."[9] Gerty continued her struggle to obtain a faculty position until 1947, when she was appointed professor of biochemistry. That same year, she and Carl shared a Nobel Prize in medicine for effecting the first synthesis of glycogen in a test tube. As the third woman, and first woman from the United States, to receive the Nobel Prize, Gerty Cori continued her research and eventually discovered that genetic disease can result from a defective enzyme.[10]

Still, women scientists were making more progress in areas related to nutritional needs of the family and the science of the care of the home. Icie Gertrude Macy Hoobler, PhD (1892-1984) was a pioneer in the scientific study of the nutritional needs of infants and children, providing the scientific community with accurate guidelines for feeding children. Her parents had encouraged her to complete her education eventually earning a PhD in physiological chemistry from the Sheffield Scientific School of Yale University in 1920. After two years as an instructor at the University of California, Berkeley, she accepted a position as director of the Nutrition Research Project at the Merrill-Palmer School for Motherhood and Child Development and the Children's Hospital of Michigan in Detroit. The project was "directed toward improving and extending scientific and technological aspects of safe and responsible childbearing and child rearing and to accumulate new and improved knowledge concerning the needs for safe motherhood." Her assignment was to "organize, equip, and direct the Nutrition Research Project as a support to the teaching and training program. It was to add a new area and service role in the community."[11] Her interest in the health and nutritional needs of women and children grew as evidence continued to accumulate that suggested the mother's diet affected the development of the fetus. The Nutrition Research Project, successor to the Children's Fund of Michigan, initiated a campaign to study and educate women on proper prenatal nutrition. Among their research findings were that breast milk is superior to commercial formulas, and they pinpointed the metabolic activity of healthy children.[12]

The scientific study of nutrition was gaining in popularity as a field open to women. Agnes Fay Morgan (1884-1968) was a biochemist whose research addressed practical problems of nutrition and food chemistry, particularly the vitamin contents of cooked and uncooked vegetables. In 1936, she established the Department of Home Economics at the College of Letters and Science at the University of California, Berkeley. Here she introduced scientific human nutrition courses, and was the first to make chemistry and biochemistry an integral part of the curriculum.[13]

The consequences of nutritional deficiencies were being examined and identified throughout the world. In England, Cicely Williams (b. 1893) was a physician who, while working in Africa, initially gained her reputation while working in Africa as the first person to describe Kwashiorkor Disease, a nutritional disorder associated with insufficient protein intake. Her interest in children prompted her to launch a major campaign against feeding sweetened condensed milk to babies. Perhaps her most challenging crusade, however, was to provide health education to effectively reduce disease. Her message was simple and straightforward: it was criminal to take a child to a hospital, cure his disease, and promptly return him to the same unhealthy environment which bred the disease in the first place. She contended that by using lay health support staff to supervise the family's involvement in follow-up care, much could be done to eliminate the cause of many childhood diseases. Above all, she stressed, it was important to listen to the people in the community in order to provide them with adequate health information.[14]

The information available to consumers was confusing, however. How could one be sure they were providing healthy meals for their families? Lydia Roberts (1879-1965) was a nutritionist who contributed practical applications of knowledge on protein, vitamin, and mineral requirements. As a long-time member of the Council on Food and Nutrition of the American Medical

Association, she was elected in 1943 to head the committee to establish the nation's first recommended daily allowances of nutrients. She had obtained her Bachelor of Science in Home Economics at the University of Chicago in 1917, when she was age 38. In 1923, she earned her Master of Science degree while serving as assistant professor of home economics at the University. In 1927, she wrote the classic *Nutrition Work with Children* which was the first book to include a basic understanding of child nutrition and the application of educational procedures. She became so well-respected for her work in nutrition that she was selected in 1929 to serve on three committees of the White House Conference on Child Health and Protection, including the committee on nutrition. By the time she was asked to work out guidelines for the daily allowance of nutrients it was wartime. Her leadership abilities were needed to establish recommendations for the addition of vitamins and minerals to flour and bread as a measure to improve the nutritional value for a nation struggling through a world war.[15]

World War II ended abruptly in 1945, when the atom bomb was dropped on Hiroshima, and later Nagasaki, Japan. Now the world had entered a new age–filled with the fear that man himself could ultimately destroy mankind. At the same time, however, no one could deny the effect such advanced knowledge could have on the well-being of the world's population. X-ray and diagnostic technology was improving, but it was Helen Taussig, MD (1898-1986) who developed the first x-ray diagnostic technique for the heart. Working with Alfred Blalock, MD, Taussig specialized in correcting malformations of the heart. Together they spearheaded the development of cardiac catheteritization and angiocardiography. She was the first physician to recognize the causes of pulmonary stenosis in children and convinced Dr. Blalock to assist her in developing a surgical technique to prevent the deaths of "blue babies." *Congenital Malformations of the Heart* (1947) was the basis on which pediatric cardiology was formed, and encouraged many young physicians to enter the new and demanding field.[16]

Endnotes Chapter 10

1. Sicherman, *Notable American Women, The Modern Period*, p. 614.

2. O'Neill, ed., *The Women's Book of World Records and Achievements*, p. 216.

3. Raven and Weir, *Women of Achievement*, p. 232.

4. Uglow, ed., *The International Dictionary of Women's Biography*, p. 184.

5. Raven and Weir, *Women of Achievement*, pp. 227-228.

6. E. T. Williams and Helen M. Palmer, *The Dictionary of National Biography*, pp. 575-576.

7. *Ibid.*

8. Sicherman, *Notable American Women, The Modern Period*, pp. 651-652.

9. *Ibid.*, p. 166.

10. *Ibid.*

11. Icie Gertrude Macy Hoobler, *Boundless Horizons, Portrait of a Pioneer Woman Scientist*, p. 84.

12. *Ibid.*, pp. 96-101.

13. Rossiter, *Women Scientists in America*, pp. 200-203.

14. Sally Craddock, *Retired Except on Demand, The Life of Dr. Cicely Williams*, pp. 62-72, 182-193.

15. Rossiter, *Women Scientists in America*, pp. 200-203.

16. Dan G. McNamara, "Helen B. Taussig, the Original Pediatrist Cardiologist," *Medical Times*, 1978; 11:23-27.

Chapter 11

Feminism Comes of Age
1950-1975

The years between 1950 and 1975 were tumultuous with great scientific developments as well as terrific disappointments marking the readjustment period following World War II. Science had finally exceeded anyone's wildest dream. The Aswan Dam was built to control the Nile River, and atomic power was becoming a reality. Insecticides were now available to prevent destruction of crops by insect infestation.

But these same major accomplishments also produced unforeseen problems. The two superpowers, the United States and the USSR, expanded their armament capacity and entered into the Cold War. Greater antagonism was seen in other countries as well; the emerging African nations and the industrialized nations; the Arab world against the Christian/Judaic world; Communism versus free enterprise; and traditionalists against scientists.

In medicine, new vaccines could now prevent most known communicable diseases. In the 1950's Margaret Pittman, PhD (b. 1901) was responsible for standardizing the pertussis vaccine virtually wiping out whooping cough, a terrible disease that claimed the lives of many children until her development. She continued her involvement in various international and national organizations and conducted research on the treatment of meningitis. Her vaccine research included prevention of typhoid and neonatal tetanus.[1]

By now, laboratory procedures had become fairly sophisticated and researchers were learning how to accurately diagnose almost all known bacterial diseases and antibiotics were available to treat them. "By the mid-1950s, molecular biology had swept the biological world by storm. It appeared to have solved the problem of life. It brought to biology a different world of inquiry, and a different model of scientific explanation."[2] Barbara McClintock, MD (b. 1902) was a pioneer in the fields of genetics and molecular biology who discovered that chromosomes exchange genetic information and physical characteristics when they crossover in the early stages of miosis. This discovery proved to be a cornerstone in the field of genetic study. In 1951, she discovered that genes are not fixed but actually move around inside the body. She concluded that the genes that determine such characteristics as color are manipulated by genetic "controlling elements" whose locations on chromosomes are not fixed.[3]

The study of genetics was further enhanced thanks to the work of Rosalind Franklin, PhD (1920-1958). She was a physical chemist and molecular biologist in England, who first described the probable structure of the DNA molecule, which made possible the successful construction of a DNA model created by James Watson and Francis Crick in 1953. Her family was supportive of her desire to become a scientist, but were concerned about the problems she might face professionally. She graduated from Cambridge in 1941, and continued her research there as investigator of gas phase chromatography. In 1942, she joined the British Coal Utilization Research Association where she studied the physical structure of carbonized coals. In 1947 she moved to Paris and went to work at Labortorie Central des Services Chnimique de l'Etat Pas where she developed her skill in x-ray diffraction techniques. When she returned to London in 1951 to join the Medical Research Council at King's College, she was able to apply the techniques she had learned in Paris to the problems of the structure of DNA.[4] In 1953, she began working on the problems of virus structure by using the helical structure. Her contribution to Watson and Crick was crucial in providing them with vital data for the DNA structure. It is generally believed that, had she not died prematurely of cancer, she would have shared with them the Nobel Prize.

Also doing important work at Cambridge at this time was Dorothy Crowfoot Hodgkin, PhD (b. 1910). A biochemist who had been raised in

Egypt, she was known for her development of the x-ray method of determining the crystal structure of chemical compounds such as penicillin, Vitamin B12, and insulin. Her discovery aided the ability to artificially create these important medicines. In 1964, the culmination of years of research came when she was awarded the Nobel Prize for Chemistry and in 1965, when she became the second woman awarded Britain's Order of Merit.[5]

Radiation continued to hold great promise in the treatment of disease, but determining a safe level was difficult. Biophysicist Edith Hinkley Quimby, PhD (b. 1891) had spent years warning the public about the dangers of exposure to radiation. Between 1920 and 1940, she publicized the correct dosages of radium for treating cancer patients. "For decades Quimby patiently measured the results of various forms of radiation, making it possible to determine the exact dosages to be used in radiology."[6] In 1958, she co-authored, *Radioactive Isotopes in Medicine and Biology*, and two years later wrote *The Safe Handling of Radioactive Isotopes in Medical Practice.*

Also working in the field of radiation research was Rosalyn Yalow, MD (b. 1921) who, in 1959, together with her partner Solomon Berson, developed the radioimmunoassay, a test that allowed precise measurement of certain substances in the blood that were previously undetectable. Dr. Yalow was teaching at Hunter College when the young nuclear physicist was introduced to Edith Quimby in 1947.[7] After their first meeting she became involved with setting up the radioisotope lab at the Bronx Veteran's Administration hospital. It was there she began her 22-year partnership with Berson, in which they eventually shared the Nobel Prize for medicine in 1977. "Radioimmunoassay was a very important discovery. If one considers that for many years half the papers from the Endocrine Society and many from other medical society meetings were dependent on radioimmunoassay, it is evident that the Nobel Prize in 1977 was appropriate," said Dr. Yalow. "What delayed our getting the Nobel for so long was the fact that it took a while to catch on that this was a very basic tool for investigation in many areas of medicine."[8]

While these new and exciting areas opened up it seemed the possibilities were endless in science and medicine. Smallpox, measles, scarlet fever, syphilis, and poliomyelitis had been brought under control in the Western world. The public began to have unrealistically high expectations for successful results in all medical situations. As a medical officer in the US Food and Drug Administration, Frances Kelsey, MD (b. 1914) refused to bow to public and the manufacture's pressure, however, when in 1960 she refused to approve the commercial use of a new hypnotic drug called thalidomide. Although Helen Taussig was the first physician to alert the public to the horrors of the new drug, it was Dr. Kelsey's steadfastness that prevented a national disaster after it was discovered that when taken in the early stages of pregnancy, the drug could cause severe birth defects in children. This controversy accentuated public awareness of the dangers of introducing new drugs without proper clinical trials. Strict controls were established by the FDA to regulate the introduction of new drugs, especially in pregnant women.[9]

In the early 1960's it seemed man could achieve anything. But it was ecologist Rachel Carson (1907-1964) who asked at what cost progress should be made. In 1962, her book *Silent Spring* created an overnight awareness of the problems of man-made chemicals and pollutants. "Rachel Carson warned that if industrial spraying [of pesticides] continued to be uncontrolled, a silent spring would dawn, unrelieved by the song of birds or the leaping of fish in streams."[10] As a child growing up in Pennsylvania, Rachel developed an appreciation of nature while taking long walks in the woods with her mother. She was a solitary child who excelled in writing. In 1925, while attending Pennsylvania College for Women in Pittsburgh, she took a course in biology that fueled her interest in the natural sciences. She graduated in 1929 as a *magna cum laude* in zoology and went to work at the Marine Biological Laboratory at Woods Hole, Maryland. It was here that she developed her special interest in the ocean and marine life. In 1931, she taught at the University of Maryland and, in 1932, she received her Master's degree in zoology and genetics at Johns Hopkins University. In 1936, she was appointed an aquatic biologist with the US Bureau of Fisheries. Within five years the bureau merged with the Bureau of Biological Survey to become the US Fish and Wildlife Service and promoted Rachel to Editor-in-Chief of the new organization's publications division. She was responsible for the bureau's publication of 12 booklets on *Conservation in Action*. "In these booklets,

Carson decried the unnecessary waste of natural resources in the United States, and called for a responsible nationwide policy of conservation to prevent a permanent depletion or extinction of wildlife."[11]

In addition to her work for the bureau, she spent her free time working on her manuscript, *The Sea Around Us* (1952), which depicted the scientific and historical aspects of the ocean and it's inhabitants. The book was an instant success and remained on the best-seller list for 86 weeks.[12] Her success let her resign from the bureau to concentrate on writing. She followed her book with *The Edge of the Sea* (1955), which also captured the public's attention. It wasn't until 1957, when her neighbors reported disastrous environmental effects from anti-mosquito pesticide, that she first became interested in this new threat to the Earth's ecology. "For the next four-and-a-half years, Rachel Carson stockpiled evidence showing how modern technology and agri-business were destroying the natural world." *Silent Spring* provided the impetus for the environmental movement in the United States and Rachel Carson, despite failing health, lobbied state legislatures and initiated 42 bills to limit the use of harmful pesticides.[13]

By the middle of the decade women were proving themselves quite capable researchers and scientists. Elizabeth Crosby (1888-1984) was an educator in neuroanatomy and one of the first to outline the evolutionary history of the brain by carefully describing the physical structure of the brains of reptiles and other vertebrates. After receiving her PhD from the University of Chicago in 1915, she taught at the University of Michigan and by the time she retired from academia in 1959, she had participated in writing many important books on neuroanatomy.[14]

The mid-1960's brought also a new openness to talk about women's issues not previously addressed in public. While birth control had been practiced for centuries, it still was not accepted wholeheartedly by the medical community. As medical director of Planned Parenthood Federation of America (PPFA) Mary Steichen Calderone, MD (b. 1904) established the organization as a leader in the birth control movement. Accepting the position at age 50, she was instrumental in developing the PPFA into a well-respected organization with the support of the medical profession.[15] But planning parenthood wasn't enough, thought Dr. Calderone after her resignation from the PPFA in 1964. At the PPFA, she was concerned with population control, but one thing that was lacking was an understanding of sex. "People never have sexual intercourse in order to have babies, people have intercourse to have *pleasure*," she thought to herself. "You love each other, so what is wrong with pleasure? How can we deny it so fiendishly when it's universal. . . .There *has* to be a way of legitimizing sex, not just by the marriage ceremony, but legitimizing the *being* of sex." Between the years 1959 and 1963, she toured the country lecturing groups on the subject of sex as a natural and normal function. In 1964 she founded the Sex Information and Education Council of the United States (SIECUS) dedicated to teaching a wary public about their own sexuality.[16]

As women became more comfortable with their own sexuality and their right to pursue their educational goals, clearly their own self-confidence was opening doors in the health-care field. But as difficult as it had been for white women to assimilate into a white male-dominated profession, it was all the more difficult for a black woman to achieve the level of success now being attained by her white counterparts. Jane C. Wright, MD (b. 1909) followed in the footsteps of her father, a black surgeon who graduated from Harvard Medical School, and who spent much of his career devoted to cancer research. She received her medical degree from New York Medical College in 1945 and served her internship at Bellevue Hospital. She completed her residency at Harlem Hospital where she eventually became the clinician for the Cancer Research Fund. Her research in cancer therapy and chemotherapy led to several national and international awards for her contributions to cancer research.[17]

Progress was being made in extending the lives of cancer patients, but one area of social awareness had not been broached. Most people could not talk openly about death and dying and once it was assumed no more could be done for a patient medically, virtually nothing was done to enhance his or her quality of life. Cicely Saunders, MD (b. 1918) was a nurse, and later a physician, who took a particular interest in her patients that were near death. One patient especially caught her attention, and in the few short weeks she knew him, she fell deeply in love with him. David Tasma's death in 1947 brought to her the realization that more must be done to recognize the needs of the dying. Years later, she again fell in love with a patient, but he touched her in a different way. Now she knew that a separate hospital devoted to care for the dying had to be established. It was with this in mind that, in 1961, she established St. Christopher's, the first Hospice. The edict was simple: the facility would be used to promote research; encourage the training of doctors and nurses on care of the dying; to provide care not only in the hospice, but the patient's home as well; and have available a small chapel or church for Christian worship.[18]

The emotional aspects of death were also addressed late in the 1960's when Elisabeth Kübler-Ross, MD (b. 1926) published her book *On Death and Dying*, (1969). Patients who would previously have not been told of their illnesses, were now encouraged to discuss their fears with family and friends, and to take care of unfinished business. Death was no longer a taboo subject. Her book detailed the five stages of death–denial, anger, bargaining, depression, and finally, acceptance. Perhaps it was a result of her early life in a concentration camp that caused Dr. Kübler-Ross to take such an interest in patients once thought to have been helpless. She noted as a child that children who anticipated death spontaneously drew butterflies on the walls. From that experience she concluded that "dying is life coming out of a cocoon."[19]

By the 1970's the feminist movement had broken down many of the remaining doors barring women's advancement and it was not considered unusual to see a woman in any job a man could perform. Although they still could not command the same salaries men did, the slogan "equal pay for equal work" was starting to have some impact. Women continue to influence world health as they obtain more powerful positions in all facets of medicine, law, and the allied health fields.

Endnotes Chapter 11

1. *Who's Who in Science*, p. 1352.

2. Evelyn Fox Keller, *A Feeling for the Organism: The Life and Work of Barbara McClintock*, p. 4.

3. *Ibid.*

4. Uglow, ed., *The International Dictionary of Women's Biography*, p. 182.

5. *Ibid.*, p. 226.

6. Weiser and Arbeiter, *Womanlist*, p. 132.

7. Lynn Gilbert and Galen Moore, *Particular Passions, Talks with Women who Have Shaped Our Times*, p. 47.

8. *Ibid.*, p. 44.

9. Weiser and Arbeiter, *Womanlist*, p. 140.

10. Marlow, *The Great Women*, p. 336.

11. *Ibid.*, p. 335.

12. *Ibid.*

13. *Ibid.*

14 "Elizabeth Crosby: Laying the Foundations of Neuroscience," *Research News*.

15. Gilbert and Moore, *Particular Passions, Talks with Women who Have Shaped Our Times*, p. 257.

16. *Ibid.*

17. Shirley du Boulay, *Cicely Saunders, Founder of the Modern Hospice Movement*, pp. 55-73.

18. *Ibid.*

19. Elisabeth Kübler-Ross, *On Death and Dying*, pp. 10-34, 139-160.

Bibliography

Abram, Ruth J., "Daughters of Aesculapius," *Journal of the American Medical Women's Association*, 38; 3:71-72, 82.

Abram, Ruth J., ed., "Send Us a Lady Physician," *Women Doctors in America, 1835-1920*, New York, W.W. Norton, 1985.

Addams, Jane, *Twenty Years at Hull House*, New York, The Macmillan Company, 1914.

Agonito, Rosemary, *History of Ideas on Women*, New York, G. P. Putnam's Sons, 1977.

Barnes, Bart, "Helen Taussig, Doctor for Blue Babies Dies," *The Washington Post*, May 22, 1986:B10.

Bauer, Carol, and Lawrence Ritt, "The Little Health of Ladies, An Anatomy of Female Invalidism in the Nineteenth Century," *Journal of the American Medical Women's Association*, 36; 10:300-306.

Beauvour, Simone de, *The Second Sex*, trans. H. M. Paisley, New York, Alfred A. Knopf, 1975.

Bird, Caroline, *Enterprising Women*, New York, Mentor, 1976.

Boulay, Shirley du, *Cicely Saunders, Founder of the Modern Hospice Movement*, London, Hodder and Stoughton, 1984.

Bridenthal, Renate and Claudia Koonz, *Becoming Visible, Women in European History*, Boston, Houghton Mifflin, 1977.

Buckmaster, Henrietta, *Women Who Shaped History*, New York, Collier, 1986.

Burns, Edward McNall, Philip Lee Ralph, Robert E. Lerner, Standish Meacham, *World Civilizations*, 6th ed., New York, Norton, 1982.

Calloway, Doris Howes, "Nutrition Research By and About Women," *Journal of the American Dietetic Association*, 84; 6:642-648.

Carson, Rachel, *Silent Spring*, New York, Fawcett Crest, 1962.

Cartwright, Frederick F., *Disease and History*, New York, Thomas Y. Crowell Company, 1972.

Castiglioni, Arturo, *A History of Medicine*, trans. E. B. Krumbhaar, New York, Alfred A. Knopf, 1941.

Chicago, Judy, *The Dinner Party*, Garden City, New York, Anchor Books, 1979.

Cowan, Ruth Schwartz, Ellen Swallow Richards: *Technology and Women*, Cambridge, Mass., MIT Press, 1981.

Craddock, Sally, Retired Except on Demand, *The Life of Dr. Cicely Williams*, Oxford, Green College, 1983.

Crankshaw, Edward, *Maria Theresa*, New York, Viking Press, 1969.

Davis, Marianna W., ed., *Contributions of Black Women to America*, volumes I & II, Columbia, SC, Kenday Press, Inc., 1982.

Dictionary of Scientific Biography, New York, Scribner & Sons, 1973.

Dolan, Josephine, A., *History of Nursing*, 12th ed., Philadelphia, Saunders, 1968.

Douglas, Emily Taft, *Margaret Sanger: Pioneer of the Future*, New York, Holt, Rinehart and Winston, 1970.

Ehrenreich, Barbara & Deidre English, *Witches, Midwives, and Nurses, A History of Women Healers*, Glass Mountain Pamphlet No. 1, Old Westbury, NY, The Feminist Press, 1972.

Encyclopedia Americana, International Edition, Danbury, Conn., Grolier, Inc, 1983, 1990 eds.

Encyclopedia Britannica, Chicago, 1965, 1990 eds.

Encyclopedia of World Biography, Chicago, 1975 ed.

Flaceliere, Robert, *Daily Life in Greece at the time of Pericles*, trans. Peter Green, New York, The Macmillan Company, 1965.

Flexner, Eleanor, *Mary Wollstonecraft, a Biography*, New York, Coward, McCann & Geoghegan, 1972.

Frieden, Betty, *The Feminine Mystique*, New York, Dell, 1964.

Garrison, Fielding H., *An Introduction to the History of Medicine,* 4th ed., Philadelphia, Saunders, 1929.

Geis, Frances and Joseph Geis, *Women in the Middle Ages,* New York, Thomas Y. Crowell, 1978.

Gilbert, Lynn and Galen Moore, *Particular Passions, Talks with Women who Have Shaped Our Times*, New York, Clarkson N. Potter, Inc., 1981.

Gillespie, Charles C., ed., *Dictionary of Scientific Biography*, vol. 7, New York, Scribner & Sons, 1972.

Grosskurth, Phyllis, *Melanie Klein, Her World and Her Work*, New York, Alfred A. Knopf, 1972.

Grun, Bernard, *The Timetables of History,* New York, Simon & Schuster, 1963.

Haber, Louis, *Women Pioneers of Science*, New York, Harcourt Brace Jovanovich, 1979.

Hays, Maxine D., "The Impact of Women Physicians on Social Change in Medicine: The Evolution of Humane Health Care Delivery Systems," *Journal of the American Medical Women's Association*, 36; 2:82-83.

Hoobler, Icie Gertrude Macy, *Boundless Horizons, Portrait of a Pioneer Woman Scientist*, Smithtown, NY, Exposition Press, 1982.

Hume, Ruth Fox, *Great Women of Medicine*, New York, Random House, 1964.

Inglis, Brian, *A History of Medicine*, Cleveland, The World Publishing Company, 1965.

James, Edward T. and Janet W. James, *Notable American Women, 1607-1950, a Biographical Dictionary*, Cambridge, Mass., Harvard University Press, 1971.

Jex-Blake, Sophia, *Medical Women, a Thesis and a History*, Edinburgh, Oliphant, Anderson & Ferrier, London, Hamilton Adams & Co., 1886.

Keller, Evelyn Fox, *A Feeling for the Organism, The Life and Work of Barbara McClintock*, San Francisco, W. H. Freeman and Company, 1936.

Keller, Helen, *The Story of My Life,* Garden City, NY, Doubleday, 1954.

Kirchner, Walther, *Western Civilization to 1500,* New York, Barnes & Noble Books, 1960.

Kübler-Ross, Elisabeth, *On Death and Dying,* New York, Macmillan, 1969.

Leeson, Joyce and Judith Gray, *Women in Medicine,* London, Tavistock Publications Limited, 1978.

Logan, Rayford W. and Michael R. Winston, *Dictionary of American Negro Biography,* New York, Norton, 1982.

Longford, Elizabeth, *Eminent Victorian Women,* New York, Alfred A. Knopf, 1981.

Lopate, Carol, *Women in Medicine,* Baltimore, Johns Hopkins University Press, 1968.

Lovejoy, Esther Pohl, *Women Doctors of the World,* New York, Macmillan, 1957.

Macksey, Joan and Kenneth Macksey, *The Book of Women's Achievements,* New York, Stein and Day, 1975.

MacNamara, Dan G., "Helen B. Taussig, the Original Pediatric Cardiologist," *Medical Times,* 1978; 11:23-27.

Manton, Jo, *Elizabeth Garrett Anderson,* New York, E. P. Dutton & Co., Inc., 1965.

Marks, Geoffrey and William K. Beatty, *Women in White,* New York, Scribner & Sons, 1972.

Marlow, Joan, *The Great Women,* New York, A & W Publishers, Inc., 1979.

Marquis, ed., *Who's Who of American Women,* 14th Edition, Chicago, 1985-1986.

Mattfeld, Jacquelyn A. and Carol G. Van Aken, eds., *Women and the Scientific Professions,* The MIT Symposium of American Women in Science and Engineering, Cambridge, Mass., MIT Press, 1965.

McElroy, Janice E., ed., *Our Hidden Heritage,* Pennsylvania Women in History, Washington, DC, Pennsylvania Division of the American Association of University Women, 1975.

McHenry, Robert, ed., *Liberty's Women,* Springfield, Mass., Merriam, 1980.

_____, *Famous American Women: a Biographic Dictionary from Colonial Times to the Present*, New York, Dover, 1983.

McKown, Robin, *Heroic Nurses*, New York, Putnam & Sons, 1966.

Mead, Kate Campbell Hurd, *A History of Women in Medicine from the Earliest Times to the Beginning of the Nineteenth Century*, Haddam, Conn., Haddam Press, 1977.

O'Faolain, Julia and Lauro Martines, eds., *Not in God's Image,* New York, Harper Row Torchbooks, 1923.

Ogilvie, Marilyn Bailey, *Women in Science*, Cambridge, Mass., MIT Press, 1986.

O'Neill, Lois Decker, ed., *The Women's Book of World Records and Achievements*, New York, Da Capo Press, 1979.

Opfell, Olga S., *Lady Laureates, Women Who Have Won the Nobel Prize*, Metuchen, NJ, Scarecrow Press, 1978.

Pfaffman, Mary, "Frances Stern," *Journal of the American Dietetic Association*, 24; 2:110-111.

"Paracelsus," *The New Encyclopaedia Britannica,* Chicago, Encyclopaedia Britannica, 1989.

Partnow, Elaine, ed., *The Quotable Woman From Eve to 1799,* Bicester, England, Facts on File Publications, 1985.

_____, *The Quotable Woman 1800-1981*, New York, Facts on File, Inc., 1982.

Perse, Teri, "The Birth Control Movement in England and the United States: the First 100 Years," *Journal of the American Medical Women's Association,* 40; 4:119-122.

Phelan, Mary Kay, *Probing the Unknown, The Story of Dr. Florence Sabin,* New York, Dell Books, 1969.

Pizan, Christine de, *The Book of the City of Ladies*, trans. Earl Jeffrey Richards, New York, Persea Books, 1982.

Raven, Susan and Alison Weir, *Women of Achievement,* New York, Harmony Books, 1981.

Rayner, William B., *Wise Women: Singular Lives that Helped Shape Our Century*, New York, St. Martins Press, 1983.

Rhodes, Philip, *An Outline History of Medicine*, London, Butterworths, 1985.

Rosenthal, Perihan Aral and Judith Eaton, "Women MDs in America: 100 Years of Progress and Backlash," *Journal of the American Medical Women's Association*, 37; 5:129-133.

Rossiter, Margaret W., *Women Scientists in America, Struggles and Strategies to 1940*, Baltimore, The Johns Hopkins University Press, 1982.

Sayer, Anne, *Rosalind Franklin and DNA*, New York, W.W. Norton, 1975.

Sicherman, Barbara, *Alice Hamilton, A Life in Letters*, Cambridge, Mass., Harvard University Press, 1984.
Sicherman, Barbara and Carol Hurd, eds., *Notable American Women, the Modern Period*, Cambridge, Mass., Belknap Press, Harvard University Press, 1980.

Singer, Charles and E. Ashworth Underwood, *A Short History of Medicine*, New York, Oxford University Press, 1962.

Strasser, Susan, *Never Done, a History of American Housework*, New York, Pantheon Press, 1982.

Tannahill, Reay, *Sex in History*, London, Abacus Editon, Sphere Books Limited, 1981.

Thomas, Caroline Bedell, "Fulfilling the Promise: Hopkins Women before World War II," *Journal of the American Medical Women's Association*, 36; 2:40-43.

Thomas, Henry and Dana Lee Thomas, *Living Biographies of Famous Women*, Garden City, New York, Garden City Books, 1959.

Toddhunter, E. Neige, "Biographical Notes from a History of Nutrition: Sarah Tyson Rorer," *Journal of the American Dietetic Association*, 42; 1:75.

Truman, Margaret, *Women of Courage*, New York, Morrow, 1976.

Turner, Thomas B., "Women in Medicine, a Historic Perspective," *Journal of the American Medical Women's Association*, 36; 2:33-37.

Uglow, Jennifer, ed., *The International Dictionary of Women's Biography*, New York, Continuum, Publishing Company, 1982.

Walker, Kenneth, *The Story of Medicine*, New York, Oxford University Press, 1955.

Wallechinsky, David and Irving Wallace, *The Book of Lists*, Bantam Books, 1977.

_____, *The People's Almanac*, Garden City, NY, Doubleday, 1975.

Walsh, Mary Roth, "Doctors Wanted: No Women Need Apply," *Sexual Barriers in the Medical Profession*, 1835-1975, New Haven, Conn., Yale University Press, 1977.

Warner, Deborah Jean, "Women in Science in Nineteenth Century America," *Journal of the American Medical Women's Association*, 34; 2:59-62.

Weiser, Marjorie P. K. and Jean S. Arbeiter, *Womanlist*, New York, Atheneum, 1981.

Westkott, Marcia, *The Feminist Legacy of Karen Horney*, New Haven, Conn., Yale University Press, 1986.

Whitman, Alden, ed., *American Reformers*, New York, The H. W. Wilson Company, 1985.

Williams, E. T. and Helen M. Palmer, *The Dictionary of National Biography*, New York, Oxford University Press, 1981.

Wilson, Dorothy Clarke, *Lone Woman: The Story of Elizabeth Blackwell*, Boston, Little Brown, 1970.

Wollstonecraft, Mary, *The Vindication of the Rights of Woman*, New York, Penguin, 1982.

Woloch, Nancy, *Women and the American Experience*, New York, Alfred A. Knopf, 1984.

Woolf, Virginia, *A Room of One's Own*, New York, Harcourt Brace Jovanovich, 1979.

Biographical Index

Addams, Jane (1860-1935)	United States	Social Reformer
Agnodice (fl. 506 BC)	Greece	Physician
Anderson, Elizabeth Garrett (1836-1917)	England	Physician
Aspasia (ca. 2nd c.)	Rome	Surgeon
Baker, Sara Josephine (1873-1945)	United States	Physician
Barry, James (1793-1865)	England	Surgeon
Barton, Clara (1821-1912)	United States	Humanitarian
Beecher, Catherine (1800-1878)	United States	Teacher/Lecturer
Bingen, Hildegard of (1099-1179)	Germany	Medical Writer
Bissell, Emily (1861-1948)	United States	Humanitarian
Blackwell, Elizabeth (1821-1910)	United States	Physician
Blackwell, Emily (1826-1910)	United States	Administrator
Bourgeois, Louise (1553-1636)	France	Midwife
Calderone, Mary Steichen (b. 1904)	United States	Physician
Calenda, Lauria Constantia (fl. 15th c.)	Italy	Physician
Carson, Rachel (1907-1964)	United States	Conservationist
Cellier, Elizabeth (fl. 1680)	England	Midwife
Chinchon, Ana de (fl. 17th c.)	Peru/Spain	Countess
Cleopatra (ca. AD 100)	Rome	Physician/Writer
Comnena, Anna (1083-1148)	Constantinople	Physician
Cori, Gerty (1896-1957)	United States	Physician
Crosby, Elizabeth (1888-1984)	United States	Neuroanatomist
Curie, Marie (1867-1934)	France	Scientist
Dick, Gladys (1881-1963)	United States	Scientist
Dix, Dorthea (1802-1887)	United States	Social Reformer
Duges-LaChappelle, Marie (1769-1821)	France	Midwife
Evans, Alice (1881-1975)	United States	Researcher
Fabiola (d. 399)	Rome	Physician
Franklin, Rosalind (1920-1958)	England	Chemist
Freud, Anna (b. 1895)	England	Psychoanalyst
Garrett, Mary Elizabeth (1854-1915)	United States	Philanthropist
Hamilton, Alice (1869-1970)	United States	Physician
Hodgkin, Dorothy Crowfoot (b. 1910)	England	Biochemist
Hollingsworth, Leta S. (1886-1939)	United States	Psychologist

Hoobler, Icie G. M. (1892-1984)	United States	Nutritionist
Horney, Karen (1885-1952)	United States	Psychologist
Jacobi, Mary Putnam (1842-1906)	United States	Physician
Jacobs, Alleta (1849-1929)	Holland	Physician
Jex-Blake, Sophia (1840-1912)	England	Physician
Jonet-Duges, Marie (1730-1797)	France	Midwife
Keller, Helen (1880-1968)	United States	Social Reformer
Kelley, Florence (1859-1932)	United States	Lawyer
Kelsey, Frances (b. 1914)	United States	Physician
Kenney, Elizabeth (1886-1952)	Australia	Nurse
Klein, Melanie (1882-1960)	England	Psychiatrist
Kübler-Ross, Elisabeth (b. 1926)	United States	Physician
Lakey, Alice (1857-1935)	United States	Community Leader
Lathrop, Julia (1858-1932)	United States	Social Reformer
Lathrop, Rose Hawthorne (1851-1926)	United States	Nurse
Lee, Rebecca (fl. 1860's)	United States	Physician
Leporin-Erxleben, Dorthea (1715-1762)	Prussia	Physician/Author
Maass, Clara (1876-1901)	Cuba	Nurse
Macy, Anne Sullivan (1866-1936)	United States	Teacher
Mance, Jeanne (1606-1673)	Canada	Physician
Manzolini, Anne Morandi (1716-1774)	Italy	Professor
Maria Theresa (1719-1780)	Austria	Queen
Marillac, Louise de (1591-1661)	France	Humanitarian
McClintock, Barbara (b. 1902)	United States	Physician
Mears, Martha (fl. 1790's)	England	Midwife
Merit Ptah (ca. 2500 BC)	Egypt	Physician
Montagu, Mary Wortly (1689-1763)	England/Turkey	Humanitarian
Morgan, Agnes Fay (1884-1968)	United States	Biochemist
Nightingale, Florence (1820-1910)	England	Nurse
Pennington, Mary Engle (1872-1952)	United States	Researcher
Piscopia Elena (1646-1684)	Italy	Doctor
Pittman, Margaret (b. 1901)	United States	Researcher
Pizan, Christine de (1363-1431)	France	Author
Quimby, Edith Hinkley (b. 1891)	United States	Researcher
Richards, Ellen Swallow (1842-1911)	United States	Chemist
Roberts, Lydia (1879-1956)	United States	Nutritionist
Rorer, Sara Tyson (1849-1937)	United States	Dietitian
Sabin, Florence Rena (1871-1953)	United States	Physician
Sanger, Margaret (1879-1966)	United States	Nurse
Saunders, Cicely (b. 1918)	England	Physician
Sharp, Jane (b. 1620)	England	Midwife
Slye, Maud Caroline (1869-1964)	United States	Physician
Sophia of Scandinavia (fl. 16th c.)	Scandinavia	Queen
Stern, Frances (1873-1947)	United States	Dietitian
Stopes, Marie Carmichael (1880-1958)	England	Social Reformer
Stowe, Harriet Beecher (1811-1896)	United States	Author

Taussig, Helen (1898-1968)	United States	Physician
Theodora (508-548)	Constantinople	Empress
Trotula Platerius (1050-1097)	Italy	Physician/Teacher
Walker, Mary (1832-1919)	United States	Physician
Williams, Anna Wessels (1863-1954)	United States	Bacteriologist
Williams, Cicely (b. 1892)	England	Physician
Wollstonecraft, Mary (1759-1797)	England	Author
Woolf, Virginia, (1882-1941)	England	Author
Wright, Jane C. (b. 1909)	United States	Physician
Yalow, Rosalyn (b. 1921)	United States	Physician
Zakrewska, Marie (1829-1902)	United States	Physician

Index

Achaean League   4, 7
Addams, Jane   59-60
Afghanistan   35
Agnodice   3, 4
Alexandria   11
Alexiad   14
Alexis I   14
American Child Health Association
                                      66
American College of Obstetricians
    and Gynecologists   71
American Federation for the Blind 67
American Home Economics
    Association   56
American Medical Association   71
Council on Food and Nutrition   83
American Red Cross   53, 68
Association of   53
American Revolution   27
American Statistical Society   46
American Women's Educational
    Association   41
Amsterdam, Holland   57
Amundsen, Roald   77
Anatomy   2, 7, 15, 21, 22, 24, 30-31,
           36-37, 44, 56, 49-50, 54
Anesthesia   37
Angiocardiography   84
Anthony, Susan B.   41, 49
Apothecaries Act   36
Arabia, Arabs   9, 12, 13, 87
Aristotle   4, 7, 13, 15, 21
Army Nursing Corps   47
Asia   4
Aspasia   8
Association for the Advancement of

Psychoanalysis   79
Association of Medical Education of
    Women   50
Astrology   14, 31
Astronomy   19
Aswan Dam   87
*Atlas of the Medulla and the
    Mid-brain, An*   78
Atom bomb   84
Atomic power   87
Australia   35, 80
Austria   30, 72, 79

Babies' Welfare Association   66
Baclava   45
Bacteriology   58, 78
Baker, Sara Josephine   66
Bangs disease   68-69
Barry, James (Miranda Stuart)   37-38
Barton, Clara   47, 53
Beecher, Catherine   40-41
Bell, Alexander Graham   67
Berlin, Germany   78
Berlin Psychoanalytic Institute   79
Bern, University of   53
Bernard, Claude   47
Berson, Solomon   89
Bible   20
Biochemistry   56, 81-83
Biology   36, 55-56, 58, 88, 90
Birth control   8, 24, 31, 57, 70-72,
                                   91-92
Bissell, Emily   68
Black Death, *see* Plague
Blackwell, Elizabeth   44-45, 49
Blackwell, Emily   45

Blackwell, Samuel 44
Blalock, Alfred 84
Blue babies 84
Board of National Popular Education, The 41
Bologna, University of 30
Bonaparte, Napoleon 2, 35
Book of the City of Ladies, The 20
Boston Dispensary, The 73
Boston, Massachusetts 55
Bourgeois, Louise 22-23
Brisbane, Australia, Medical Society of 80
British Army 37, 46
British Association for the Advancement of Science 36
British Coal Utilization Research Association 88
British Medical Association 6
British Medical Service 37
Bronx Veteran's Administration Hospital 89
Brucellosis 68-69
Bryn Mawr 57-58
Budapest, Hungary 78
Bureau of Biological Survey 90
Byennius, Nicephorus 14
Byrd, Admiral Richard 77
Byzantine Empire, Byzantium 9, 11, 14

Caesarean section 38
Calderone, Mary Steichen 91-92
Calenda, Lauria Constantia 20
California, University of, at Berkeley 82-83
Cambridge, England, University 88
Cambridge, Massachusetts 39
Canada 25,38
Cancer 59, 68, 81, 89, 92
Cancer Research Fund 92
Candid Advice to the Fair Sex on the Subject of Pregnancy 31
Cape of Good Hope 21
Carbohydrate metabolism 81-82
Cardiac catheterization 84
Caribbean 63

Carson, Rachel 90-91
Catholic church 16, 19-22, 27, 72
Cellier, Elizabeth 24
Charities, charitable contributions 35, 68
Charlemagne 13
Charles V, of France 20
Charles VI, of Brunswick 30
Chaucer 16
Chemistry 15, 28,36, 55-56, 58, 68, 79, 83, 89
Chicago, Illinois 56, 59, 64
    University of 81, 83, 91
Child labor 36, 60, 67
Children, child rearing 78, 82
Children's Fund of Michigan 82-83
Children's Hospital of Michigan 82
Children's Welfare Federation 65
China 16, 35
Chinchon, Countess Ana de 23-24
Christians, Christianity 7-9, 13, 87, 93
Christmas Seals 68
Chromosomes 68, 88
Circulation 15
Civil War 43-51, 63
Cleopatra 8
Cold War 87
Colombian Exposition 56
Columbus, Christopher 20
Communications 36, 53
Communist party, Communism 87
Comnena, Anna 14
Comnena, John 14
Compleat Midwife Companion, The 24
Congenital Malformations of the Heart 84
Congressional Medal of Honor 47
Conservation 91
Conservation in Action 90
Constantine 9
Constantinople 11, 12, 14
Copernicus 21
Cori, Carl 81-82
Cori, Gerty 81-82
Cranford Village Improvement

Association   69
Crick, Francis   88
Crimea   45-46
Crimean War   43-51
Crosby, Elizabeth   91
The Crusades   14
Curie, Marie   69-70
Curie, Pierre   69-70

Darwin, Charles   46
Daughters of Charity   23
Death, thoughts on   2, 11, 92-93
De Fabrica Corporis   21
Delaware   68
Diabetes   68
Dick, George   74
Dick, Gladys   74
Dickens, Charles   36
Die gross Wundartzney   21
Diet   3, 7, 24, 73-74
Dietetics   55-56, 73-74
Diphtheria Bacillus   58
Diseases   2, 3, 7, 11, 14, 21,
                 28, 36, 63-64, 68-70,
                 79-80, 83, 87-89
Dix, Dorthea   38-40, 47
DNA   88
Duges, Marie Jonet, see Jonet-Duges,
    Marie
Duges-LaChappelle,
    Marie Louise   29-30

East Aurora Academy   56
Ebers Papyrus   2
Ecology   55, 90-91
Ederle, Gertrude   77
Edge of the Sea, The   91
Edinburgh, Scotland   27
    University of   37, 54
Hospital for Women and
    Children   54
Education   1, 11, 13, 19, 20, 24,
                 30, 32, 40-41, 48,
                 51, 56, 59, 72-74,
                 77, 82, 92
Egypt, Egyptians   1-4, 12, 89
Elizabeth, Queen of Austria   30

Elizabeth I, Queen of England   22
Endocrine Society   89
Energy   69
England   19, 22, 24, 25, 29,
                 31, 35-37, 43, 45-46,
                 50, 53, 54, 72, 77,
                 79, 83, 88
Environment   68, 91
Eton College   19
Europe   4, 11, 13-14, 16, 19,
                 21, 22, 24, 25, 28,
                 36, 43, 45-46, 49,
                 53, 59-60, 63-64, 71
Evans, Alice   68-69

Fabiola   8-9
Family Limitations   71
Federal Children's Bureau   65
Female Medical College
    of Pennsylvania   50
Feminist movement   40, 51, 72, 92
Ferdinand V, King of Spain   20
Food preparation   56, 73
Food Research Laboratory   73
Ford, Henry   64
Fracastorius, Hieronymus   21
France   25, 32, 43, 48, 50
Franco-Prussian War   43-51
Franklin, Rosalind   88
Frederick, of Prussia   30
French Revolution   27
Freud, Anna   78-79
Freud, Sigmund   78-79
Frieburg, University of   79

Galen   7, 13, 21
Galileo   21-22
Gama, Vasco da   21
Garrett, Mary Elizabeth   57-58
Gas phase chromatography   88
General Federation of Women's
    Clubs   69
Genetics   68, 82, 88, 90
Geneva (New York)
    Medical School   44
Geneva Treaty   53
German University,

Medical School of 81
Germany 9, 15, 19, 43, 54
Glycogen 81-82
Gods and goddesses 1-3, 7
Great Depression 79
Greece, Greeks 2-4, 7, 8, 13
Gutenburg, Johann 20
Gynecology, *see* Obstetrics and
gynecology

Halle, University at 30
Hamilton, Alice 64-65
Handicapped, treatment of 23, 67
Harlem Hospital 92
Hartford Female Academy 40
Harvard University 51
    School of Medicine 65, 92
    School of Public Health 65
Hawthorne, Nathanie 58-59
Hebrews 13
Henry VIII, of England 21
Heredity 47, 81
Hildegard of Bingen 15
Hippocrates of Cos 3, 13
Hippocratic oath 3, 24
Hiroshima, Japan 84
Hodgkin, Dorothy Crowfoot 88-89
Holland 30, 57
Hollingsworth, Leta S. 72-73
Home economics 41, 55-56, 73, 83
Hoobler, Icie Gertrude Macy 82-83
Horney, Karen 79
Hospice 58, 93
Hotel-Dieu (Montreal) 25
Hotel Dieu (Paris) 29
    Hull House 59-60, 64-66
Hull House Maps and Papers 60
Hunter College 89
Hygiene 3, 8, 14-15, 22, 31

Illinois Board of Charities 65
Illinois State Bureau of Labor 60
Indian Sanitation Commission 46
Industrial Poisons in the
    United States 65
Industrial Revolution 31, 35
Infant mortality 30, 65

Infantile Paralysis and Cerebral
    Diplegia–Methods Used for
    Restoration and Function 80
Influenza 22, 28
Insecticides 87
Institute of Radium 70
International Committee of
    the Red Cross 53
Isabella I, Queen of Spain 20
Islam 11, 12
Italy 13, 22

Jacobi, Mary Putnam 50-51
Jacobs, Aletta 57
Jex-Blake, Sophia 53-54
Joan of Arc 20
John, King of France 16
Johns Hopkins 58, 78, 90
Jonet-Duges, Marie 29
Journal of Home Economics 56
Justinian 11
Juvenile deliquency 60, 65-66

Karolinen Children's Hospital 81
Keller, Helen 67
Kelley, Florence 60
Kelsey, Frances 90
Kenney, Elizabeth 80-81
King's College 19, 88
Klein, Melanie 78
Koch, Robert 58
Kübler-Ross, Elisabeth 93
Kwashiorkor Disease 83

Labortorie Central des Services
    Chnimique de l'Etat Pas 88
LaChappelle, Marie Louis Duges, *see*
    Duges-LaChappelle, Marie Louis
    29, 30
Lake Placid, New York, 56
La Materité 44
Lancet, The 36
Lathrop, Julia 65
Lathrop, Rose Hawthorne 58-59
Laws of Life with Special
    Referenceto the Physical
    Education of Girls, The 44

Lead poisoning 65
Le Dirie sur Jejanne d'Arc 20
Lee, Rebecca 48
Leeuwenhoek, Anton van 23
Leipzig University 19
Leporin-Erxleban, Dorthea 30
Le livre de la citë des dames 20
Liber Compositae Medicinae 15
Liber Divinorum Oiperum 15
Lindbergh, Charles 77
Linneaus, Carolus 28
Lister, Joseph 46
"Little Curies" 70
London, England 27, 4, 48, 50, 53,
60, 72, 78, 88
London School of Medicine
for Women 50, 53-54
London University 50

Maass, Clara 63
Macy, Anne Sullivan 67
Macy, John 67
Magellan, Ferdinand 21
Malaria 24, 28, 58, 63
Malta 38
Mance, Jeanne 25
Manzolini, Anne Morandi 30-31
Maria Theresa, Queen of Austria 30
Marillac, Louise de 23
Marine Bilogical Laboratory 90
Married Love 72
Maryland, University of 90
Massachusetts 39
Massachusetts Institute of
Technology (MIT) 48, 54-55
Massachusetts State Board
of Health 55
Materia medica 2
Maxwell, Clerk 47
McCall Pattern Company 65
McClintock, Barbara 88
Mears, Martha 31
Medical education 1, 11, 13,
30,49-51
Medical licensing 29
Medical practice 11-13, 15, 16, 20,
28, 29, 44, 50-51

Medicine, medical knowledge
1, 2, 4, 12, 14,15, 21,
24, 25, 35-37, 43,
48-49, 53, 58, 63,
77-78, 80, 89, 92
Medici, Queen Marie D' 22
Medicis, The 22
Mendel, Gregor Johann 47
Mental illness 23, 39, 65
Mental institutions 27, 38-40
Merit Ptah 1
Merrill-Palmer School for
Motherhood and Child
Development 82
Methodism 27
Metrodora 8
Michaelangelo 22
Michigan, University of 64, 91
Microscopy 36
Middle Ages 11-16
Middle East 12
Middlesex Hospital 49
Middlesex House of
Corrections 38-39
Midwives, midwifery 22-24,
29-31, 66
Miller, Albert 47
Miranda, General Francisco 37
Miss Beecher's Domestic
Recipe Book 40
Mohammed 12
Montagu, Lady Mary Wortley 29
Montreal 25
Morgan, Agnes Fay 83
Muslims 12

Nagasaki, Japan 84
National Academy of Sciences 77
National Association for the
Advancement of Colored
People (NAACP) 60
National Consumer's League
50, 60, 69
National Tuberculosis
Association 68
Nature 19, 69
Neuroanatomy 91

New Century Cooking School 56
New England 25
New England College for Women
   and Children 54
New England Female
   Medical College 48
New England Kitchen 56
New Jersey Women's Association 69
   New York City Health
   Department, Division of
   Child Hygiene 66
New York College of Pharmacy 50
New York Infirmary for Women
   and Children 45
   Women's Medical College of 50
New York Milk Committee 69
New York Psychoanalytic
   Institute 79
New York State Institute for the
   Study of Malignant Diseases 81
New York University's
   Bellevue Medical School 67, 92
Newton, Isaac 22
Nightingale, Florence 45-46
Nightingale School 46
Nile River 1, 2, 87
Nobel Prize 69-70, 82, 88-89
North Pole 77
Norway 23
Nosocomium 9
Nurses, nursing 45-46, 58-59, 73
Nutrition 65, 73, 78, 82-84
Nutrition Research Project 82
Nutrition Work with Children 84

Observations 22
Obstetrics and gynecology 1, 3, 8, 13,
   15, 22, 23, 29-31
Occupational disease 64
Occupational Disease
   Commission 64
On Death and Dying 93
On Diseases of Women 13
Order of Merit 46, 89
Origin of the Species 46
Otto the Great 13
Oxford University 15

Padua, University of 24-25
Panama Canal 63
Paracelsus 21
Pare, Ambroise 21, 22
Paris, France 23, 25, 30, 45, 50,
   69-70, 77, 88
Paris University 15
Pasteur, Louis 46-47
Pasteurization 47, 69
Pathology 2, 28, 36, 51, 78, 81
Paul, Vincent de 23
Pediatric cardiology 84
Pennington, Mary Engle 73
Pennsylvania College fo Women 90
Pennsylvania, University of 56, 73
Peru 23
Peruvian bark 23
Pesticides 91
Philadelphia Cooking School 56
Physica 15
Physics 19, 28, 36, 58, 69-70
Physiology 15, 28, 44, 51, 56
Pilgrims 27
Piscopia, Elena 24
Pittman, Margaret 87
Pizan, Christine de 20
Plague 12, 14, 16, 22, 23
Planned Parenthood Federation
   of America 91-92
Plato 3
Polio patients 80
Poliomyelitis 80, 89
Polo, Marco 15-16
Population growth 28, 43, 70,
   84, 92
Pregnancy, *see* Obstetrics and
   gynecology
Prison system reforms 38-39, 57
Protestant revolt 27
Psychoanalytic Institute 79
Psychosomatic medicine 51
Public health 29, 35, 36, 43, 67, 73
Pure Food and Drug Act 69, 73
Pure food movement 69
Putnam, George Palmer 50
Quakers 27

Queen's College 54
Queensland, Australia 80
Quimby, Edith Hinkley 89
Quinine 24

Radcliffe College 67
Radiation therapy 89
*Radioactive Isotopes in Medicine
and Biology* 89
Radioimmunoassay 89
Radium 69, 89
Reconstruction 48
Registration Act 36
Religious beliefs 2, 11, 14,15,
19, 23, 25
The Renaissance 8, 19-25
Rhazes of Basra 12
Richards, Ellen Swallow 54-56
Roberts, Lydia 83-84
Rockefeller Institute 78
Rockford (Ill.) Seminary 59
Roman Empire, Rome 4, 7-9, 11
Room of One's Own, A 79
Rorer, Sarah Tyson 56-57
Royal Humane Society 27-28
Royal Society 31
Royal Statistical Society 46
Rumford Kitchen 56
Russian Royal Scientific Society 31

Sabin, Florence Rena 77-78
*Safe Handling of Radioactive Isotopes
in Medical Practice, The* 89
St. Bartholomew's Hospital 44
St. Christopher's Hospice 93
St. Jerome 8
St. Mary's Dispensary for Women 49
St. Rose's Free Home for Incurable
Cancer 59
St. Thomas Hospital 46
Salerno Medical School 13-14, 20
Salvation Army 48
Sanger, Margaret 70
Sanitation, sanitary
engineering 23, 35, 36, 38,
45, 55, 60, 64
Sauders, Cicely 92-93

Scarlet fever 28, 74, 89
Science 2, 4, 7, 12, 15, 21,
27, 35-36, 44, 48-49,
53-54, 56, 68, 70,
73, 77-78, 80, 82, 89
Scurvy 16, 22, 29
Scuturi, Turkey 45
Sea Around Us, The 91
Servants of Relief for
Incurable Cancer 59
Servitus, Miguel 21
Sex education 92
Sex Information and Education
Council of the United
States, (SIECUS) 92
Sharp, Jane 24
Silent Spring 90-91
Simmons College 56
Slavery 36, 47
Slee, Noah 71
Slye, Maud Caroline 81
Smallpox 12, 22, 28, 29, 31,
43, 89
Social awareness 27, 35-36, 48, 59
Social Security Act 67
Socialist Party, Socialism 60, 71
Socrates 3
Sophia, Queen of Scandinavia 23
Sorbonne 50, 70
South Africa 35, 38
South Pole 77
Spain 23, 24
Spanish Inquisition 36
Stanton, Elizabeth Cady 41, 49
Starr, Ellen 60
Statistical data 29, 46
Stern, Frances 73-74
Stone, Lucy 49
Stopes, Marie Carmichael 71-72
Story of My Life, The 67
Stowe, Harriette Beecher 40
Stroud, William 41
Surgery 8, 14, 20, 21, 29, 37
Switzerland 53
Sydenham, Edward 24
Syphilis 22, 68, 79, 89
Syracuse Medical College 47

Tasma, David 92
Taussig, Helen 84, 90
Technology 48, 63
Temple of Sais 1
Thalidomide 90
Theodora 11
Theodosius 9
Thoughts on Education of Daughters 32
Thoughts on Education of the Fair Sex 30
Toynbee Hall 60
Transportation 35, 53
Travel 27, 35
Travels with Marco Polo 16
Treatise on Domestic Economy 40
Treatise on Electricity and Magnetism 47
Trotula Platerius 13-14, 22
Tuberculosis 14, 16, 22, 58, 64, 69
Turkey 29
Typhoid, typhus 28, 45, 64, 87

Uncle Tom's Cabin 40
Union Pacific Railroad 48
United States 36, 43, 44, 47, 50, 53, 58-59, 63-64, 71-72, 79, 81, 87
United States Army 47
United States Bureau of Fisheries 90
United States Department of Agriculture (USDA) 69, 73
United States Fish and Wildlife Service 90
United States Food and Drug Administration (FDA) 90
The Universe 19, 21
USSR 87

Vaccines, vaccinations 29, 43, 58, 87
Valley of the Tombs of the Kings 1
Vaselius, Andreas 21
Vassar College 55
Victoria, Queen of England 35, 46

Vienna, Austria 30
Vinci, Leonardo da 22
Vindication of the Rights of Woman, The 32
Visigoths 9, 11
Vitamins 79, 83-84, 89
deficiency of 29, 79

Walker, Mary 47-48
Washington University School of Medicine 82
Waterloo, Battle of 35, 37
Watson, James 88
Watt, James 31
Western Female Academy 40
White House Conference on Child Health and Protection 84
Whooping cough 87
Wiley, Harvey 69
Williams, Anna Wessels 58
Williams, Cicely 83
Wise Parenthood 72
Witches, Witch hunts 24
Wollstonecraft, Mary 32
The Woman Rebel 71
Women's Medical Association of New York 50
Women's Medical College at Northwestern 64
Women's Medical College of Pennsylvania 56, 59
Women's rights 32, 48-49, 67, 70
Woods Hole, Maryland 90
Woolf, Virginia 79
World War I 65
World War II 84, 87
Wright brothers 64
Wright, Jane C. 92

X-rays 69-70, 84, 88-89

Yale University, Sheffield Scientific School of 82
Yalow, Rosalyn 89
Yellow fever 63-64, 68

Zakrewska, Marie 45